FAITHSONG
A New Look
at the Ministry of Music

FAITHSONG
A New Look
at the Ministry of Music

THOMAS L. ARE

The Westminster Press
Philadelphia

Scripture quotations from the Revised Standard Version of the Bible are copyrighted 1946, 1952, © 1971, 1973 by the Division of Christian Education of the National Council of the Churches of Christ in the U.S.A., and are used by permission.

Scripture quotations from *The New English Bible* © The Delegates of the Oxford University Press and The Syndics of the Cambridge University Press 1961, 1970, are reprinted by permission.

Book Design by Alice Derr

First edition

Published by The Westminster Press®
Philadelphia, Pennsylvania

PRINTED IN THE UNITED STATES OF AMERICA
9 8 7 6 5 4 3 2 1

TO
CHORISTERS GUILD—that Texas crowd who does
more than anyone else I know to minister to
the Minister of Music

Library of Congress Cataloging in Publication Data

Are, Thomas L., 1932–
  Faithsong : a new look at the ministry of music.

  1. Music in churches. 2. Church music—United States.
3. Church music—Protestant Churches. I. Title.
ML3001.A73   264'.2   81-4789
ISBN 0-664-24375-4   AACR2

Contents

This book is not about singing—
It's about *RELATIONSHIPS*.
It is not about music—
It's about *MINISTRY*.
It is not about ideals, ideas, or dreams—
It's about something very real,
It's about *YOU!*

Preface

For most jobs in the church there is a support system. In my denomination, if you serve as a Sunday school teacher or adviser to young people, help abounds. On a presbytery, synod, or General Assembly level you will find at least one job-related packet that says, "This is what the job involves, these are the goals, and here are some resources." But that's not true for the minister of music.

Church musicians are the most neglected of all professionals. They are crowded into an all-too-small rehearsal room, given an all-too-small budget, an enormous task, and lots of "good lucks."

They often fail! We wonder why.

Many denominations have no office or officer committed to helping local choir directors do a better job. Each congregation, left to its own resources, reaches out into the community to bring in the best leadership it can find. Some churches do very well. Others, desperate for a musician, will hire almost anyone who can beat out a melody on the piano. Preparation for the ministry of music may involve little more than playing trombone in the college band; but if one can handle "Come to Jesus" in the key of C, a position as director of the music program of the local church may be waiting. Even so, when such persons fail, it is often not because of poor musicianship but because of role confusion.

Some choir directors don't have the foggiest idea of what the church does, or its purpose for being—and some aren't the least bit interested in finding out. No wonder we refer to the choir loft as the "war department" of the church.

On the other hand, some ministers see music as no more than a filler in the service of worship. They see the church musician as a hired hand employed to lead the music program. The idea that an organist or a choir director is, in fact, also in ministry and committed to the tending of souls never enters their minds.

After working closely with choir directors for twenty years, I am convinced that many of them are hurting. They are confused about their role in ministry and uncertain as to where to turn for help. They do not fully belong to the ranks of the clergy, nor are they laity. And they feel alone.

This book is for them, the choirs they lead, and the clergy with whom they serve. It is written with the conviction that the church musician, professional or part-time, is called, first of all, to ministry. And whatever musical skills one has can be used in ministry to people.

Some of the basic concepts discussed in Chapters II and IX appeared in my book, *My Gospel of Stewardship*, 1977, published by Lay Renewal Publications, Tucker, Georgia. They are enlarged upon here with permission of the publisher.

T.L.A.

Prelude:
Music in Ministry

*If music is to be effective in the mission of the church, the faith
of the singer must be expressed in the song.*

We cannot separate the faith of the preacher from the
sermon, nor the faith of the Sunday school teacher from the
lesson. Neither can we separate the faith of the singer from the
song. *Faithsinging sings the singer's faith.*

For too long we in the church have been training theologians
in one room and musicians in another. We bring them together
for the first time at eleven o'clock on Sunday morning and
wonder what has gone wrong with worship.

We have made better progress in other areas. In my
denomination it took us nearly a century to learn that we
couldn't copy our program of Christian education after the
public schools. For years we thought if we did it like the pros, we
would really get it done. Then one day we realized that we deal
with a living Holy Spirit. It is not enough for us to communicate
facts. If we are serious about our faith, we must also provide a
context in which we might have an experience with God now.
We explain our new understanding by saying that education
must not only be a *witness* to what God has said but it must also
be an *instrument* through which God speaks today.

For fifteen years I have been convinced that the church
needs also to rethink the whole area of music. *Sacred music
must not be only a witness, it must be also an instrument.*

Music as a witness is vital. But music that simply recalls the faith of others is not enough. To gather on Sunday morning around reproduced anthems is insufficient. Sacred music must provide the context for us to experience and express our faith here and now. We create music, we never just reproduce it.

There is a difference between music as an art and music as an instrument for spiritual growth. Music as an art is an end in itself. It begins with the C-major scale. It has to do with notes, rhythm, and tone. On the other hand, music as an instrument of spiritual growth begins on our knees. It grows out of faith and devotion, and is, at best, a means to an end.

Denominational leaders who advise the church in the area of music to "tap the resources of the pros" scare me. For when we speak of music as an instrument of spiritual growth, many of the pros have little idea of what we are talking about.

I don't minimize the importance of Sunday morning music. But what happens on Thursday night during choir practice or Saturday morning with the children's choir is equally important. Singers relate to one another in rehearsal. And for sacred music, *relationship is more important than performance*. The message we perform is precisely that we are dependent upon God and interdependent upon one another.

Music has power. The reason we use a certain brand of toothpaste or drive the make of automobile we drive is that some good-looking person or group on television advises us in song to do so. We run out and buy that kind. The slogan of advertisers is true: "If you want to sell it, sing it."

Industrialists understand the power of music. They play it in factories and have a 20 percent efficiency increase. A New York insurance firm declared that when music is piped into their records room, they have a 19.3 percent decrease in typing errors. Doctors use less Novocain because of music.

Even agriculturists use music. Bell Laboratories reports that corn grows faster to the sound of the flute.

I read in the newspaper about a Texan who claims to grow

the biggest tomatoes in his county. He does this not by pouring 10-W-30 on them. He said, "Every day when I get home from work, I stroll down to the garden and *sing to 'em.*"

The Purina people say that when they play music in their barns, their hens lay bigger and better eggs. That's power!

Entertainers also use music. Not only Lawrence Welk and Engelbert Humperdinck but soap operas too. The only way networks can produce those programs in thirty minutes (with thirty commercials) is with special music effects. At points of high drama, a distinct organ swell sounds—and presto, they have grabbed our attention. It fills the house as though shouting: "Quit ironing now, Momma, this time we're going to announce who the father of that baby really is. If you miss it now, it may be weeks before we get back to it!"

Someone discovered the power of music and everybody uses it. Music is a part of all that we are: a part of our history and our heritage; of our theology, worship, promise, and faith; and of our very beings. We in the church need to use it with greater understanding.

The Bible is filled with music. Prick the Scriptures almost anywhere and hymns of praise burst out. King David appointed four thousand ministers of music for the Temple (I Chron. 23:5). On the toughest night of his life, before going out into the Garden of Gethsemane, Jesus and his disciples sang a hymn (Matt. 26:30).

Paul says, "I will sing with the heart and sing with the understanding also" (I Cor. 14:15b). I haven't counted the passages, but it has been claimed that the Bible has more to say about music and singing than it has to say about preaching and prayer.

Music reflects our history. Every time the church has moved forward, that advance has been accompanied by new music. From the time the early Christians marched into the arena singing for courage and spiritual strength to the freedom marches of Martin Luther King, the work of the church has been accompanied by music. Whether it was Luther's great "Ein' feste Burg," or the voice of Ira Sankey singing "There Were Ninety and Nine" which could be heard a block away, or "We Shall Overcome" of the 1960's, music has stirred the emotions and directed the mind. From spirituals to rock, music has taught the Christian in the church and on the street.

As a pastor, most of what I try to do in ministry is accompanied by music. Look at it:

1. *Worship.* One of my main responsibilities is conducting worship. The most fundamental relationship in life develops between us and God as we worship. In worship we learn who we are. Music dominates more than half of the average church service.

The human heart is naturally cold to God. The Bible compares our hearts to clay, in need of molding. When I enter a sanctuary on Sunday morning, I'm not ready to worship. Other thoughts flood my mind, such as, With all I have to do, what am I doing here? I enter the sanctuary somewhat detached.

But then I become aware of a new atmosphere created by the architecture, the gathering of people, and the *sounds of music.* I hear the prelude. The choir sings "O come, let us worship and bow down," and I join in the singing of an uplifting "Joyful, Joyful, We Adore Thee." I can no more help warming up to God than I can help becoming hot in the sunshine.

The Bible tells us of certain ways in which God makes himself known to us. I believe music is one of them. It is a spiritual sunshine, a basic means of worship.

2. *Christian Education.* Every year I buy books on theology. As a pastor, I can't do without them. Yet when it comes to what I really believe about God, much of my faith does not come from books. It grows out of what I began to experience

with God in my early years sitting around campfires on youth retreats, scratching red bugs and singing spiritual songs about God and his love.

Music has a power to communicate thoughts too deep for words and emotions too deep for reason. Someone has said if I can write the hymns, it makes no difference who writes the theology, the masses will go with me.

3. *Evangelism*. Music isn't just heard, it is experienced. We are "moved" not only by its message but even more by the effect of its total sound upon us as emotional persons. In every congregation there are those who have come into the church because they have experienced the music program. In the congregation I serve it is not unusual for prospects to enter into the life of the church for the first time through the choir.

One of the evangelistic successes in our church is through children involved in choirs. When I first started in the ministry, I served a dual role. I directed the choirs on Sunday morning and I preached for the Sunday night service. We often had as many people in church at night as we did for the eleven o'clock service. I thought they came because of my preaching. Then it became evident that on the nights when the junior choir did *not* sing, our attendance dwindled. What a blow to my ego to realize that the enlarged congregation was coming to hear them, not me.

A youngster has no hesitation in cornering an uncle or a neighbor. "Our choir is singing in church tonight, will you come hear me sing?" Some critic might challenge this by saying, "They are not coming for the right reasons." But if they come for any reason and if we do our jobs effectively as worship leaders, some will stay. Besides that, I know of no one who went to church the first time for all the right reasons. We are still glad they came.

4. *Fellowship*. Nothing unites a crowd more quickly than singing together. Joining in a song even calms rowdy

youngsters in a classroom. I have seen high schoolers, charged up from recreation, quickly prepared for worship by the use of music.

Children change from talking about the church where their parents belong to speaking of "my church" when they see their names in choir robes. Give them opportunities to lead the congregation in worship and the church becomes theirs.

Music permeates all we seek to do as a church. Yet, in spite of the power and importance of music, some church leaders will consider it as little more than a filler. A colleague of mine once said: "Tom, you get too excited about music. Personally, I feel music is somewhat like stained-glass windows. They're beautiful if you can afford them, but if not, you haven't lost anything essential." I think it is essential. The music ministry deserves much more support than is traditionally given to it.

Christian education has been king. We spend enormous sums of money on classrooms and curriculum resources. Presbyteries, synods, and the General Assembly employ professional staff persons as Christian educators to help develop teachers and leaders in the congregations. We spare no effort to keep abreast of the latest teaching methods and curriculum development.

When I was in seminary, it seems that the unwritten doctrine was "justification by scholarship alone." The campus hero wasn't the person with a passion for service or a beautiful devotional life but the one with the highest grades.

I am not belittling Christian education. Knowledge about the faith is necessary, but it also holds limitations. I am asking for a balance. I don't know of a presbytery that employs a staff person in music or worship.

In the local church the minister of music is the last full-time person added to the staff of a larger church and the most underpaid in the smaller church. There are very few resources available to help keep abreast of the meaningful opportunities in music.

The imbalance in standards between the minister and the minister of music illustrates the gap. We require preachers to go four years to college, three to seminary, and nowadays, we frequently encourage them to return to graduate school. Church courts will not turn preachers loose on an unassuming congregation unless they are first assured that candidates have been harnessed and headed in the "right" direction. They are examined and supervised throughout years of preparation. We require similar standards for pastoral counselors and directors of Christian education.

On the other hand, we have only the vaguest standards for the minister of music. Most denominations have no school specifically preparing those who feel called to this specialized ministry. Many schools have excellent music departments, but few such schools compare to the average seminary. The closing of the prestigious School of Sacred Music at Union Theological Seminary (New York City) makes more critical the question, Where does one go to be grounded in the worship and message of the church in preparation for the ministry of music?

The most frequent explanation for the lack of vital music ministries within the average church is "lack of funds." We have demonstrated, however, that Christians will create and finance anything that we are convinced will further the Kingdom of God. It is a matter of values.

A full music ministry in the congregation where I am pastor has had no drain on the budget. Dedicated ministers of music will "pay for themselves" through new monies brought into the church as the result of their ministry. When I became the pastor of a struggling suburban Presbyterian church a controversy had divided the congregation. Presbytery's judicial action removed not only the previous pastor but also all elders and deacons. The congregation struggled with guilt and failure. Membership had decreased by 40 percent. Finances depleted and program ministries plummeted. All the vital signs: negative.

My first strategy for turning this church around was to negotiate for a full-time minister of music. "But first, we will need a new secretary and a director of Christian education" was almost the unanimous response. However, a few influential leaders who either had vision or did not want to discourage their new pastor supported my plan.

Two months later we added an exceptionally talented and committed minister of music to our staff. (It was a year and a half before we could afford a full-time janitor.)

Within a few months our minister of music had enlisted 60 percent of the families of our congregation in a music program of seven choirs and four instrumental groups. Worship attendance and giving doubled. Now we can hardly afford not to have a ministry of music. We recently built a new sanctuary. We feel our program of education and outreach rival any in the city.

I have given a brief overview of the power and importance of music for the mission of the church. Too often we have relegated music to an obscure corner and allowed it to fall asleep. We tiptoe around it for fear we might wake it up and not know what to do with all that power. I plead for an awakening of music as a powerful instrument of the worship and total mission of the church.

I No Casual Worship, Please

"I wish I enjoyed worship more, but to tell the truth, most of the time I'm just plain bored."

Jean not only spoke for herself, she was expressing the inner feelings of millions. Services of worship often produce an attitude of "Let's get this done so we can do something interesting."

Church leaders are concerned about what is happening to worship. Attendance has fallen on hard times. People are unhappy. Preaching is dull and congregations seem to be indifferent.

Church was over. Jean walked to the parking lot with her friend Martha. "I would like to be more involved. But unless you're in the choir, all you get to do is sing two hymns, recite the creed, and say the Lord's Prayer. I just lose interest." She stopped walking for a moment, looked up and spoke as though she had thought of a new hope. "Yet I still have a hunger for God. I feel worship is my link with him."

This emptiness expressed by Jean is precisely what keeps bringing us back to worship.

In worship we keep an appointment with God. He comes to us with grace, even though we are a fallen people. Without his grace we would choke on the hay and stubble type of requirements life forces on us every day. Worship unchokes us.

We can come to worship with hopes or doubts, fears or

expectations; we can come in pain or in joy. The only way we cannot approach real worship is *casually*. There are no casual hymns, or preludes, or prayers, or anthems, or offerings, or amens. Worship is love. We don't approach love casually. It is both joyful and serious.

In the late 1960's, perceptive people began to strive for renewal in worship. The old would no longer do and was declared phony or empty. They questioned whether traditional practices and symbols had contemporary meaning.

New voices were proclaiming a "post-Christian era." Some even said: "God is dead. The church is no more than an escape mechanism for the aging. Preachers should be confined to the streets. And worship—'it's meaningless.' "

Church leaders panicked. Some cried:

"Jazz it up!"

"Let the streets write the agenda."

"Put some life into it!"

"Come hear our choir. It's what's up front that counts!"

"Make the church swing, baby!"

These slogans became the battle cry of those who wanted to rescue the church from the death of dull worship.

Hope for new life was legitimate. Many shared in it. However, sometimes the means toward good ends became ends in themselves. Eager ministers and musicians began experimenting.

It is hard to believe that anyone really expected dancers in leotards and Coca-Cola Communions to become the norm for Sunday morning worship, but such things claimed our attention. Many persons in the pews deplored the "shock treatment."

Some worship leaders felt that all we needed to do was to adopt new media for communication. The Old World learned by reading. Then suddenly we were in a world of instantaneous reality. Television offered a higher degree of participation and was more emotional than a dull diet of words.

Those most hungry for new media, the synthesizer sound effects and reversed screens, were young people whom Marshall McLuhan called the "post-literate" generation. They were not so much interested in what was *said* in church. Their question was, *"What happened?"* They became bored with the lack of action. "We sing a few eighteenth-century hymns, say a creed, and pray. But nothing really happens," they said.

Yet the hope for revitalizing worship is not in "jazzing it up." Nothing is gained by substituting dull liturgy with "lit-orgy." This term is not mine but was first used by Paul Hoon in *The Integrity of Worship* (p. 298; Abingdon Press, 1971). The promise for more meaningful worship is not in faster tempo but in better understanding.

Therefore, those who lead in worship, including the choir, musical groups, or solo performers, need to have clearly in mind what worship means and their role in it.

What is Christian worship?

Remember the story of "Willie say he don't want the ball"? Let it be told another way. The score is 21–17, with Willie's team trailing in the last quarter. The quarterback hands off to Willie. He sweeps the end and starts downfield. Suddenly, two opposing tackles charge toward him. Willie steps out of bounds and keeps on running. He jumps the bench, runs up the aisle, out through the entrance gate and past the ticket taker; he runs through the parking lot, jumps the net on the tennis court, throws down the ball, and does his victory dance. Then he shouts back to the stadium, "Did I score?" Of course not. He was disqualified the moment he stepped out of bounds.

If worship is to have theological integrity, there are several boundaries that must be observed.

1. Christian worship must be a reverent *response to the Creator, God.*

In keeping with the now mood, a mod minister opened his

pastoral prayer, "Oh, great Cheshire cat, grinning in the cosmos, if you are listening, meow back to us." That's too far out of bounds to score.

The question we must ask is, What kind of God does our worship reflect? Our style of worship reflects our understanding of the character of God. What we believe determines what we pray and how we sing. Worship is not happy ignorance, nor a means of trying to win God's favor. Christian worship is our joyous response to the grace of God.

The big word in worship is *response*. Before we can *express* anything in worship, we must first be *impressed* by God. "Worship can be a sacrifice man offers only when it is first seen as a sacrament God offers." (Ibid., p. 44.) Or, another way to say it is that theology precedes doxology.

Why is this distinction so important? Because corrupt impressions breed corrupt expressions. It is a matter of whether we worship God or an idol.

We cannot measure meaningful worship by, "Well, they sure seemed to like it." Worship is more than a good show. Worship may be entertaining and fun, but that is not what makes worship meaningful. Christian worship is not to be judged by its ability to titillate the emotions or to intrigue the intellect. The danger is that when the message is so identified with the medium, we proclaim the medium and ignore the message. For instance, if we worship music rather than the God music proclaims, it may sound the same, but its meaning is lost.

We are not free to worship just any way we please. God must be worshiped in ways consistent with God's revelation of himself. *God is always the creator, and the worshiper is always the creature.* Worship must always maintain a high level of dignity, reflecting respect and gratitude.

Singing of "The Man Upstairs" is a too-casual expression of God's coming to us. Of course, he does, but he comes as God, not as a buddy. Worship, most of all, celebrates the God who is indeed the omnipotent Lord of all creation. Such worship is never nonchalant.

On the other hand, we cannot mistake drabness in worship as reverence. If God indeed loves us, our response to this "good news" will reflect a high degree of excitement and joy. Apathy can hardly be an appropriate response.

2. Christian worship is *centered in Christ.*

Physicists tell us that if we are to understand human vision, we cannot simply contemplate the structure of the eye, we must first study the properties of light. That's the way it is when we seek to understand worship. We don't begin with what we do. We must open with the "properties of light" which, for the Christian, is Christ. Christ is Lord. In our adoration it is not so much that we tell him but that we listen and acknowledge.

The significance of Christ-centered worship is at least twofold.

To begin with, defining worship as "worth-ship" is too narrow. Christian worship is more than an exercise to identify the value of God. When we see worship as accrediting God, it puts too much of the initiative in our hands. The worship of God is always a response.

If anyone is ascribing worth, *it is God who imputes worth to us.* The wonder is that God cares for us: "We love, because he first loved us." This is precisely the motive for worship. Our worship is focused on God, not on us, not even the best of us, not even us to the nth degree, but on God, who creates, saves, and loves us.

Worship defined as ascribing value to nature or beauty perverts. Sometimes the musician is tempted to experience God as the God of beauty rather than the God of Christian revelation. The character of God—his holiness, his active righteousness, his moral will, his judgment, mercy, and love—is sometimes displaced by a vision of God as beauty. Yet we know there is a difference between music as art (an end in itself), and music as liturgy. The freedom enjoyed by the composer or performer in expressing individual vision elsewhere cannot prevail in liturgy. Music must be chosen for its theological truth, both in message and mood, and not for its artistic qualification alone.

Also, recognizing the presence of Christ in worship means that *the experience is personal.* Bonhoeffer writes, "Christ is not Christ in Himself, but in His relation to me . . . that is, Christ cannot be thought of in His being in Himself, but only in His relationship to me" (Dietrich Bonhoeffer, *Christ the Center,* tr. by John Bowden, pp. 47-48; Harper & Row, 1966). We have a responsibility in worship to let God be God. It is blasphemy to demand that God be something to us other than who he has revealed himself to be in Jesus Christ.

The good news is not only that we can know our salvation but that we can have fellowship with him who saves us. His promise is to be present where two or three are gathered together. Our worship is not just to a God up there but also very much to God-in-us. We may never understand, but in worship, we do experience him.

The old argument of whether choirs "sing to the Lord" or "sing for the people" is irrelevant. Of course we sing to the Lord. But we are singing to the Lord, not up there, but dwelling *in his people.* The goal of the anthem is to enable the worshiper, by emotions, insights, and aesthetics, to become more aware of the Christ within.

3. Christian worship has integrity only when *mediated by the Holy Spirit.* All the authority of theology or orthodoxy or of the preacher is superseded by the authority of the Holy Spirit, who makes worship happen. Our freedom, which has been so emphasized recently, is not license. It is a bound freedom.

The Holy Spirit is not an idea about God, nor a maverick principle. He is God himself, among us. He dwells within our fellowship and is the source of order as well as the source of freedom. Before the choir can sing in harmony with integrity, the choir members should be bound together as persons in harmony. The Holy Spirit does this binding. *If the choir cannot give itself as much to the desires of the Spirit as it does to the desires of the composer, then its song is hypocritical.* It sings of a new life it does not seek. For our music to have integrity, it must become *our* message and reflect *our* experiences.

The Spirit is the Spirit of liberty, like the wind which blows where it wills. Those who worship have freedom in response. Yet the Spirit implies not only freedom but *unity.* The Spirit desires that we love one another. The church's power is its union with its Lord and with its members. What matters is not whether worship makes us feel good or happy. What matters is whether worship makes us more Christlike.

Unity doesn't happen as the result of our determination. Unity is the result of our awareness of God. *We can love each other to the degree that we are aware of God's love for us.*

In my experience, this awareness is not a constant. It is a come-and-go kind of experience. The most significant things in life happen to us in moments. Even our awareness of God occurs in split seconds. It may touch us during the singing of a hymn or while we are repeating some well-worn phrase in a creed or prayer. It may take place with some new idea expressed in the sermon or during the trailing off of the last notes of the choir's anthem. But suddenly we are aware of the presence of God. We feel his love, we are caught up in more than a sidewalk frame of mind and see life as more than what can be recorded in the newspaper. In those brief experiences, the Holy Spirit allows us to feel at one with God and with our fellow worshipers. Perhaps that moment is more important than all the rest of the week. It gives increased meaning to all the rest of time.

Atmosphere is reason enough for spending the church's money for a sanctuary. Many multi-use buildings look more like a gymnasium than a place of prayer. We are creatures who respond to atmosphere. We will spend twice as much for a meal in a pleasant place. Whatever it costs to create the kind of context that will better enable us to have those split-second experiences of God awareness in worship seems worth it.

A sensitive person has respect for emotions. Anytime we have an awareness of God's presence, it is an emotional experience.

Some leaders of worship, however, not really convinced that the person in the pew would recognize the presence of God, decide to play it safe. They learn how to produce emotional experiences, especially with music, as proof of God's presence. Others reject this empty substitute and label it sentimentality. It is shallow and phony and divorced from reason and reality. Perhaps they overcompensate.

Emotion and reason are not in opposition to each other. The gospel is good news and our worship is an emotional response. The presence of God is known through feelings. In short, *God is felt.*

Worship is exciting and too deep for logic. It is no casual happening. It moves beyond theology. Worship becomes doxology.

II   What Happens
When We Worship?

Sunday morning, 11:23 A.M. A drunk walked through a door that opens directly into the sanctuary. He looked around, adjusted his eyes to the darkness, and suddenly realized he faced a crowd of six hundred persons. Loud and disruptively he asked, "Well, what's going on here?"

If worship is to convey meaning, we must have some idea of what is going on. Yet many worshipers and some ministers have little idea of what is supposed to be happening during the hour of public worship on Sunday morning.

The Bible has much to say concerning worship, our need for it and its practice. But we find few details about what happens when we actually do it. The most descriptive Scriptural accounting is the record of Isaiah's experience in the Temple (Isa. 6:1-8). A careful analysis of this text shows a progression that is not only theological but also psychological.

If the word "celebrate" can be interpreted as "re-creating the mood of a significant event," the Christian church has been celebrating Isaiah's experience for generations. This text shows the elements of worship and implies a psychological progression that can be shown in table form:

TEXT	ELEMENTS OF WORSHIP	PSYCHOLOGICAL PROGRESSION
I. *Recognition* "I Saw the Lord"	Sanctuary- Architecture Prelude Call to Worship	Recognition of majesty, mystery, and worth of God
II. *Praise* "Holy, Holy, Holy"	Hymn of Praise Anthem Doxology	Response to worth by expression of appreciation
III. *Confession* "Woe Is Me"	Confession of Sin Hymn or Anthem of Confession Prayers	Comparison of God's holiness to our unholiness Sense of sin, anger, and guilt
IV. *Assurance of Pardon* "This Has Touched Your Lips— Forgiven"	Scripture Sermon Hymn-Anthem	Experiencing freedom in pardon and renewed relationship
V. *Dedication* "Here Am I"	Offering Hymn Prayer Charge Benediction	Response to good news with gratitude and renewed commitment to service

I. *Recognition of the Presence of God*

In the year that King Uzziah died, Isaiah entered the Temple and said, "I saw the Lord."

The very first element of worship is the recognition of the presence of God. If we believe that God is with us, we can't help worshiping, no matter how poor the music or the sermon. On the other hand, if we are not aware of God's presence, we may have an interesting human meeting involving religious activity, but we hardly worship. Worship is our response to the presence of God.

A little boy awakened in the middle of the night, frightened and crying. He was told by his father, "It's O.K. Son, God is here with you." As Dad left the room, he overheard his son say: "If you are in here, God, please, sir, don't move. You'll scare me to death!" Some of us react that way to worship. We talk about God's presence but we are not sure we want to experience it.

We conduct most of our worship in a sanctuary. The word "sanctuary" comes from the same root as the words "sanctify" and "saint." The root means to "set aside." The sanctuary is a room set aside for worship. Surely God is everywhere but we are not everywhere aware of his presence. The building itself announces that this is the place for us to tune in to the presence of God.

Likewise, the prelude makes an announcement. It is more than a smooth covering up of the shuffle of feet. In fact, the prelude is misnamed. It is not something that happens before worship. It is very much a part of the worship experience. It announces: Now is the time to turn our thoughts and consciousness to God.

The call to worship, whether it is "The Lord Is in His Holy Temple," sung by the choir, or, "O come, let us worship and bow down," spoken by the minister, calls us to an awareness of the presence of God.

II. *Praise*

Having seen God, high and lifted up, Isaiah said the angels cried to him, "Holy, holy, holy is the Lord of hosts."

The second element of worship involves praise. Here we sing of adoration. The Gloria Patri, the Doxology, and the hymns include a call to praise. Here is the place to sing praise anthems. Those ministers who always schedule the anthem at the same place in the order of worship, regardless of its message, show little appreciation for the progression of worship. Some anthems are prayers, others are proclamation, and still others are acts of dedication. Anthems belong in their corresponding order in worship.

It is appropriate to point out that there is something also in our psyche that causes us to respond with appreciation to things of worth. We gasp when we see the Grand Canyon; we applaud performances that please; and when we "see God," something within us wants to clap hands. When we see the majesty and mystery of God, we innately respond with praise.

III. *Confession*

Isaiah's immediate response to his vision of God was "Woe is me! For I am lost; for I am a man of unclean lips, and I dwell in the midst of a people of unclean lips."

Psychiatrists tell us that comparison is an immediate human reaction. Isaiah looked up and saw God. He saw that God was holy and righteous. Immediately, Isaiah knew that he himself was not holy, but unrighteous. "Woe is me," he cried, "for my eyes have seen the King."

In the order of worship, praise is followed by a confession of sin, the acknowledgment of our humanness. This too may be expressed by anthems of confession, or by hymns such as "Dear Lord and Father of Mankind." An essential part of this element is prayer—whether silent, pastoral, or spontaneous prayers, prayer anthems, or formal printed prayers of confession.

IV. *Assurance of Pardon*

Having confessed his sins, Isaiah told that an angel flew to him with a live coal taken from the altar. The seraph said, "Behold, this has touched your lips; your guilt is taken away, and your sin forgiven."

Notice that the promise to Isaiah was not a promise that his sins would be forgiven someday in the future, but that his sins were forgiven already. It follows that the fourth element of worship is not the forgiveness of sins, but the assurance of pardon.

This is the place in worship where we proclaim the grace of God. It includes the reading of the Scriptures, the good news. A sermon proclaims God's pardon in Jesus Christ. This proclamation may also be done by the choir, in anthems; or by the congregation, in hymns. This constitutes the most difficult of all elements of worship to experience.

Call us sinners and we'll believe it. Sin awareness coincides with our experience. But proclaim redemption and we find it hard to accept. For this reason, the assurance of pardon consumes the largest segment of time in most services of worship.

V. *Dedication*

After the proclamation of forgiveness, Isaiah heard the voice of God say, "Whom shall I send, and who will go for us?" Then says Isaiah, "Here am I! Send me."

Hymns of dedication such as "Take My Life, and Let It Be Consecrated" or "O Jesus, I Have Promised" fit here. At this point, also, belong anthems of dedication. It is appropriate to take the offering here, as we give ourselves as an act of worship. We respond to pardon with gratitude and renewed commitment to service.

Most services of worship then close with the benediction and postlude. The benediction is a pronouncement of God's blessings, not a prayer. It is done from up front and with eyes open as a message is proclaimed by the King's spokesman. God has come to us with grace. We leave the worship experience uplifted, filled with his Spirit.

Several years ago a friend gave Reverend Tom Walker's young son some passes to the local circus. In their small town the circus comes once a year. The parade down main street with one elephant and one clown stirred up a lot of interest, especially in Tommy. Over and over he asked his dad, "When are we going to the circus, Daddy, when are we going?" Dad promised to pick him up at five o'clock.

When Tom walked into the house, Tommy was ready. He was so excited, he squealed and charged out the front door as if the house were falling down. Running too fast, he stumbled, rolled over, bounced back on his feet, and was jumping up and down on the front seat of the car by the time Dad got there.

Tommy laughed and jumped so high, he bumped his head on the roof. Then, as they backed out of the driveway, he sobered. With all seriousness, he asked, "Daddy, what's a circus?"

Young Tommy's excitement came, not because he knew what a circus was, but because he believed what an older friend had told him. "A circus is a place to have a good time!"

Our lack of excitement in worship comes from a lack of faith. If we believed what the Father says to us in worship, we would be jumping up and down and squealing with excitement.

Worship is mysterious and demanding. It may be too rich for us to understand. But to say that worship is dull—is unbelievable!

III Pastor and Musician as Partners

"You're needed at the hospital. Bob Murphy is having chest pains. They don't know if it's a heart attack or not. A neighbor called and thinks you should go."

After five years as his secretary, Mary already knew what Reverend Tom Walker was feeling. He faced an already impossibly crowded day. How could he take two hours for a hospital call and still get his work done?

A part of him was feeling guilty for leaving so much until the deadline. Another part was angry because yesterday was just as busy as today. So was the day before. Nevertheless, he felt responsible when he was caught like this.

Someone has said that heaven for pastors will be a completely free calendar. With no appointments all day long they can devote full time to interruptions. Maybe so, but that's not the way it is now.

Tom will go to the hospital, no matter what else he needs to be doing. "You'll have to get the bulletin done," he calls to the secretary. "Tell David I am preaching on prayer. He can pick some appropriate hymns. And tell that couple coming in at five that I'll be a little late, but I'll be here."

David Bailey drove up just in time to see Tom Walker rushing to his car. David really wanted to talk to him. In the three years he has served Westminster Church as minister of music, there never seemed to be time enough for the two of them to get together.

The glowing picture of "working together in partnership," which Tom painted when Dave interviewed for the job, has never materialized. David understands Tom's pressure, but, "Gosh, doesn't he know we can't work this way? If I am to have appropriate music ready for Sunday services, I must have some idea of a theme. After all, preparing a choir is not like preparing a sermon. The only one he has to depend on is himself. But I depend upon other people. It just can't be done at the last minute."

In honest moments David admits that he feels put down by Tom's attitude of taking him for granted. He is angry with himself, too. Just last week when Tom asked, "How's it going?" he answered, "Fine." If only he had the courage, he would have said, "Fine, except for you." But he didn't! Instead, he had muttered to himself: "He may think everything is fine. But if things don't improve, I'm going to quit!"

Dave thinks as he enters the church office, Tom had better be preaching on the cross Sunday. The choir is singing "Beautiful Saviour," and I'm not going to change.

"Oh, David, David," the secretary calls, "Tom says sing something about prayer, O.K.?"

"I won't do it!" David mumbles to himself.

With minor variations, this drama is repeated thousands of times in churches of all sizes. No matter who gives in or who makes the last-minute adjustments, the Sunday service of worship will be just as strained as the relationship between Tom Walker and David Bailey. When they miss, that is, when they fail to achieve the harmonious relationship they both want, it's tragic. The whole church feels their breakdown.

Each blaming the other gains little. In frontier days railroad tunnel diggers started on opposite sides of the mountain and dug toward each other. Sometimes they missed! Fighting over who was at fault probably released frustration, but it hardly helped the railroad. Ministers and choir directors need to commit themselves to dealing with matters far more profitable than trying to fix blame.

When these two church leaders miss each other, there are at least two factors involved: perspective and ego.

Look first at Reverend Tom Walker.

He has a strong ego. "Every good minister has," he once said. If Tom Walker didn't think he could do a better job than anyone else available, he probably wouldn't be trying to do it. Yet the same ego that enables him to perform well also gets him into trouble. Like most ministers, Tom sees himself somewhat as the hub around which the church revolves. The certainty of this importance is augmented by those who place him on a performance pedestal.

The ego of the minister is not destructive per se. All church leaders have a need for a healthy self-confidence and self-affirmation. However, when ego causes them to substitute image for function, then they are in trouble. That is, when they become more concerned about how they look in ministry than about serving others, then they lose something vital.

Tom speaks of discovering this in himself. "For years, I made hospital calls, not only because I genuinely cared for those who were sick but because I needed to be seen making hospital calls. My image of a successful pastor was of one who always made hospital calls. Patients appreciated my looking in on them and some visits even were effective. The destructive element was within me. My desire to look good often outweighed my desire to minister. These two motives, of course, are not necessarily incompatible, but at times they come into conflict. If someone failed to appreciate my visit or if the time I spent visiting caused me to neglect another responsibility, anger built up. I actually used people to feed my ego needs for a good image."

As a Christian and a minister, Tom is a paradox. He has

responded to the unconditional love of God and knows he lives by grace. At the same time a large part of him wants others to perceive him as in with God because of his excellent performance.

In spite of his words about unmerited favor, he wants to impress his parishioners with his track record. After all, as the pastor, he has been given credentials by his seminary, his church court, and the officers of his own congregation. Tom wants people to think he is in control. He would hate for others to know how important their endorsement is to him.

He, as pastor, has been officially knighted as worship expert. To prove his autonomy, the first thing he does when moving into a new church is to change the order of the service of worship.

As for music, Tom operates with two assumptions. First, he knows what the people like! Much of his attitude toward music grows out of his need to keep worshipers coming to church. He gives them what they want. They obviously expect this of him, for it is to the pastor and not to the musician that they express their taste.

One way to see what is happening to Tom is to recognize that he has an important job as pastor of a church. People look up to him. He is their leader. In order for him to perform his responsibilities as administrator, theologian-in-residence, counselor, and preacher, the officers of the church have given him certain "power roles." These powers exist mostly as images in the minds of his members; nonetheless, no minister could function without them. Tom recognizes that the authority for leadership is given to him by those who see him as a performer of ministry. Authority is identified with his role.

Tom also knows that those who give power can take it away. In large measure his leadership and power to serve as a minister depend upon how he pleases his congregation. Thus he is sensitive to their likes and dislikes. He wants the music to please them.

Second, Tom assumes that people can relate to God in a meaningful way primarily as the result of his words, his preaching. "After all," says Don Wardlaw, "beautiful feet are primarily the property of those who preach the good news." (Don Wardlaw, "Minister and Musician: Partners in Liturgy," unpublished pamphlet, p. 9; McCormick Theological Seminary, 1977.) Others lack status. Even though he knows better, Tom acts as though the only trustworthy spiritual experiences are those which can be explained. Only that which can be said in words can really be known.

He sincerely wants a better relationship with the minister of music, not only for the sake of their working together in worship but even more so because their relationship is an expression of the gospel. As "professional" Christians, Tom says, "We can only be to the world what we are first to each other." Tom wants it, but his ego gets in the way.

The thing about Tom's ego is, it is a cover-up. He is not that self-confident. Sometimes he feels like a little boy trying to fill a man's role. Inside, he is afraid. To keep himself from failure or exposure, he "plays his power." He is the manager. David, whom he respects as a competent musician, is one of those whom he must manage.

Deep down, Tom despises the role of boss. He would prefer a warmer relationship with David. To have it, though, he needs David to recognize the enormous responsibility he carries and wants David to support him. Since he is not sure David can do that, he has decided that they will have a role relationship. That means Tom = manager, David = managee. Tom will have to protect both his domain and his ego. Anything else would require a lot of trust and love and communication.

Now look at David.

The gap that separates them is widened because David, as minister of music, also struggles with perspective and ego. He expresses his ego power by seeing himself as the guardian of good taste. Since his sophomore year in college, majoring in fine arts, David has been taught that good taste is the supreme standard by which all else is to be judged. Those who were known as either having good taste or being able to recognize it were given license to be aloof from the common flock. By certain vocabulary, airs, and roles, they set themselves apart or even above others. They ensured their domain by a constant looking down upon or even ridiculing those who did not share their good taste. Of course, this judgment upon the common occurred with a degree of tolerance, but nonetheless, the status structure of "the artist" depended upon pronouncing this distinction. It established the elite.

No wonder there is a gap. Tom and David have no overriding common motivation. Tom is the worship expert. David is the music expert. Tom protects his need to please the people and the functions important to his preaching. David guards the purity of his music and the performance of his musicians.

Both those who taught David and those who hired him declared that his job was to promote great music in the church. That this job description could develop into the proverbial monkey on the church's back never crossed their minds. According to the late John Finley Williamson, founder and president of the Westminster Choir College, the call to "come into the church and encourage great music" began years ago with the invention of the talkies. Organists were no longer needed to furnish background music for motion pictures. The only other place to find employment was the church. No one else had organs. Many great ministers of music followed this route into the church and we thank God for them. Even though they "backed into" a calling to ministry, it did not detract from their great contribution to the life and mission of the church. However, in some cases, the *church became a means for producing great music rather than music becoming a means for producing spiritual growth.*

Whenever David then thinks of himself primarily as a musician and not as a minister, he is in keeping with his inherited background. An organ is used to produce sounds. It is likely then that when some musicians approach an instrument or a choir, their goal is to *use* it to produce sounds.

Unless we in the church provide support and encouragement to change the musician's orientation from production to serving people, from *performance to relationship,* we can hardly expect their concern to be for much more than good taste. And unless the minister takes time for communication around the common goal of serving people, the services of the minister and the musician will suffer.

The essential element in the relationship between Tom and David is communication. All relationships begin with communication.

On the wall in Tom's office is a poster that says:

> I know that you believe you understand what you
> think I said, but I am not sure you realize that what
> you heard is not what I meant.

Tom needs that reminder to keep him from taking for granted that just because he says something everyone understands.

Communication takes place only when there is a meeting of meanings. But what if one is preoccupied with other interests or anxious over a home situation? What if the words carry unclear connotations or the subject of conversation is emotionally loaded? Words inevitably fail. Even under the best circumstances words are often inadequate.

Someone has said that we communicate 20 percent by the words we say, 30 percent by how we say them, and 50 percent by how we look when they are being said.

What Tom says to David has to filter through Tom's images of David and Tom's image of himself.

If two persons are to work together, *they must talk.* Yet how many ministers have planning meetings with their choir directors? Church musicians complain, "I don't even know the sermon title or what hymns we'll sing until I see the bulletin on Sunday morning."

No matter how few persons are involved on a church staff, unless ministers want to be a one-person show, they need staff meetings.

Together, staff persons plan services, make announcements, air frustrations, and affirm good performance. If they do no more than touch base on individual schedules, it will be worth the efforts to hold meetings. Staff conferences also give time to brainstorm for creative ideas and to discuss goals and procedures. However, staff meetings alone are not enough for Tom and David really to become a team. Another kind of communication comes into play. It is called dialogue.

Reuel Howe said:

> Every man is a potential adversary, even those whom we love. Only through dialogue are we saved from this enmity toward one another. Dialogue is to love what blood is to the body. When the flow of blood stops, the body dies. When dialogue stops, love dies and resentment and hate are born. But dialogue can restore a dead relationship. Indeed, this is the miracle of dialogue: it can bring relationship into being, and it can bring into being once again a relationship that has died. (Reuel Howe, *The Miracle of Dialogue,* p. 3; Seabury Press, 1963)

Some students of the dynamics of communication make a distinction between discussion and dialogue. Discussion, they say, is conversation about those things intellectual, such as plans, budgets, schedules, and thoughts—the kinds of things that are mostly dealt with in staff meetings. However, real dialogue communicates on a deeper level. It is not talking about externals but sharing feelings and emotions. For effective communication to take place, a sharing of feelings must occur. "To know me, you must know my feelings," is, to my mind, a true statement.

Here are three rules for dialogue.

1. If dialogue is to occur, both parties must *listen.* This is contrary to Tom's usual pattern in conversation. Tom works hard to say just the right things. He wants to be clear. When David speaks, Tom is often thinking about what he is going to say next; he hardly listens to David. It is sometimes like the teenaged boy who came home and announced, "Mom, I've been drafted." She responded, "O.K., but be home before midnight." There is no way for us to communicate unless we make a positive effort to listen.

2. Listening for facts is essential, yet that is not enough; we must *listen to feelings.* Tom must listen not only to David's words but to his feelings. Often words deceive or cover up. Feelings speak with a truer tongue than words. The problem compounds because David has been programmed to conceal rather than to reveal. Parent figures have been telling him since he was three years old, "Big boys don't cry." That meant no matter what he felt, he had to play the man. Today, even as an adult, it is hard for him to drop his guard and let Tom really know what he feels inside. It takes love and trust for David to do that. So he plays it safe by answering, "Fine." He may be too insecure to allow himself to become vulnerable. If David exposed himself to Tom, he might be hurt by rejection or lack of understanding.

3. We must also *avoid criticism.* It seldom leads to dialogue. We don't grow when we are under attack. We dig in for defense. Even the sentence "I am telling you this for your own good" does not open blocked communication. In fact, the person David automatically avoids is anyone who has a

planned program for his improvement. He doesn't need anyone to judge him. David judges himself more severely than anyone else could. When he appears self-confident, it is a facade. His games of perfectionism, bragging, exaggerating, or cynicism are devices designed to avoid the risk of being honest or exposed. Yet his mask seldom fools anyone except himself.

David's emotions reveal who he really is on the inside, and it is only when he is accepted and affirmed that he will be able to enter into dialogue.

All these inner feelings of David's are not unique to him. They are precisely the inner feelings of Tom, too, and also of every other Tom, Dick, and Harriet in the world.

The best way to avoid dialogue is to become simply a "professional." As long as we remain the professional, we can come to church and hide. But if Tom and David relate to each other as professionals only, they are not being the church.

The church strives to be a visible expression of its message. If we fail in our relationship with each other inside the church, then to what do we have to witness?

How Tom and David love or fail to love each other is not just a matter between the two of them. They are a microcosm of the church itself. They must close the gap.

IV Pastors Are Human

Mark sells insurance. Even though he hasn't been at it long, he is a good salesman. He is bright and catches on to new things fast. He works hard. His general training was not in selling, but he genuinely cares for people and he is able in this vocation to maintain some personal relationships in business. Yet if you asked him, Mark would tell you that he is not selling insurance by choice. He does it because it is a way to feed his family.

A year ago Mark was the pastor of a six-hundred-member church. Now he has joined that ever-increasing roster of ministerial dropouts.

In seminary Mark learned to think of the church as the "mystical body of Christ." He soon found that the church he served was also an institution. It had all the classic characteristics of any other human organization. Mark learned that this heavenly body had a street address. It possessed all the problems of communication, personality conflicts, goal-setting, financial struggles, and a myriad of conflicting expectations that affect every other institution in the world.

Two years ago, while visiting with Tom, Mark had said: "Honestly, if I don't get a break soon, I don't know what I am going to do. I work six days and five nights a week. I never catch up. Getting pressure from home and criticism from the church, sometimes I get so angry I want to quit!" Last year, he did.

Tom has thought of quitting, too.

If David, the music minister, understands the pressures which the pastor faces, he has more chance to succeed in his own job. This chapter takes a look at the minister and offers a better appreciation for his role.

There is no way to write a job description for a "preacher," but certain things are obvious. First of all, Tom is a manager. His church is nearly as busy as an international airport—Sunday school, kindergarten, youth programs, women's organizations, special services, and what seems like millions of committee meetings—and Tom manages it all. He monitors one of the busiest telephones in town. He administers a budget of thousands of dollars. He spends hours reading to keep up with what's going on in the world, the community, his own denomination, new trends in theology, psychology, and current ministries of the church. He makes endless visits on prospects, the sick, those in crisis, members in hospitals, and shut-ins. Also, there are those calls "just to keep in touch."

Tom also spends hours in counseling, in both formal and informal settings. He is the resident theologian, the father of all church happenings, the local expert in evangelism, stewardship, and worship. He leads small groups, teaches communicants classes, leadership training, Sunday school, and new member classes—and eleven o'clock comes around every Sunday morning. A recent study claims that the average workweek for parish pastors is 66.7 hours (Donald P. Smith, *Clergy in the Cross Fire,* p. 79; Westminster Press, 1973).

In addition to an impossible schedule, Tom struggles with a built-in ambiguity about his authority. He is a professional whose clients are his employers. When the program of the church sags, he is held responsible, for he is the leader.

During the national economic crunch of the 1970's, several key leaders of the congregation called Tom aside. One of them said: "I don't know what needs to be done, but if you don't get the budget up, your job is in jeopardy. No matter what the circumstances, it's your responsibility to motivate this congregation to give. You're in charge here and the responsibility for what happens comes right back to your desk."

Yet if Tom moves in an unpopular direction, they quickly remind him that the officers of the church are responsible for the church's ministry; he is just an employee.

Sometimes ministry can be a grim struggle. Of all the professions, the clergy are the most under observation by their clients. Much of their performance is in public. They are expected to respond willingly to all requests for their services, day or night. "I hate to bother you on your day off but . . . ," constantly invades their private time. They seldom escape the frustrations and anxieties of a working day.

Yet Tom struggles to keep from becoming simply a professional. Although aware of Jesus' call to deny self, at the same time he can't free himself from being human.

David approached Tom one day in the hall. "I can't understand why you don't drop in on our choir rehearsals from time to time. It would help to show more interest in the music program."

Tom answered, "It's not a matter of interest, David, it's a matter of not having the time."

Walking away, David said: "Everybody has twenty-four hours a day. It's a matter of what's important."

Although true, the perspective on what's important always tempers our knowledge of the other's dilemma.

A story illustrates how we hide within our own fields. A poultry expert announced, "You farmers will get better roosters and hens if you will separate your male biddies from your female biddies." A farmer asked, "How in the world can you tell a male biddy from a female biddy?"

"It's easy," said the poultry expert. "Male biddies will eat male worms and female biddies will eat female worms."

"But how in the world can you tell male worms from female worms?"

"I don't know. I'm a poultry expert—you have to ask a worm expert about that!"

So it is with the church experts.

Ministers and musicians often pull back into their own field of expertise. Yet the hope of meaningful worship in today's church rests in the hands of pastors and church musicians who overlap in interest, support, and appreciation for both ministries.

However, before Tom can come to any realistic understanding of the role of the minister of music, he must first come to some conclusions about his own role. It will help David immensely if he can get a clear picture of Tom's outlook. After twenty years of serving as a church pastor, Tom has made some decisions about his job.

1. *The minister, alone, decides the role of ministry.*

If Tom asked twenty persons in his congregation to describe his responsibilities as they see it, he would get twenty different descriptions of what he should be doing.

In his book *Clergy in the Cross Fire,* Donald P. Smith says:

> From the first moment a young pastor steps into the pulpit or presides at a board meeting he is caught in the cross fire of conflicting expectations for the ministry. . . .
>
> If ministers preach on social issues, someone is sure to tell them to "stick to religion." If they don't, someone else will slip away from the church because they aren't relevant. . . . To fall short in any aspect of their ministry is to become the target for criticism. (Ibid., p. 13)

Through experience, Tom has learned that he will never satisfy all who have legitimate images of his task. To one, he is first of all an evangelist; thus, his job, more than anything else, is to save souls. To another, he is a preacher, and as long as he is "interesting" in the pulpit, he is O.K. Others expect him to be a priest, a social reformer, a director of effective program, an educator, a psychiatrist, a Bible scholar, or an interpreter of life. He cannot survive in the midst of all those conflicting expectations and mixed signals unless he is clear about what he expects of himself.

Parishioners all want something different. Maybe the apostle Paul was able to be all things to all people but most ministers cannot. They get lost in the maze of roles. It is more than one person can do.

Tom receives certain rewards for playing the game of super pastor-theologian-counselor-administrator-performer. As long as so much is expected of him—more than he can possibly get done—it makes him feel important! A part of him wants to keep on wearing all those masks, even if it kills him.

Ministry is a way of life and not just a means of making a living and acquiring recognition. He must trust his own feeling (which could be God's leading) and choose to do those things in ministry which are honest for him to do. Ultimately he answers only to God. He is called to serve God, not hired to work for a congregation. No one else can determine his schedule or theological stance.

Tom is human and he makes mistakes. But he does not owe it to his congregation always to be right. He owes it to them to be responsible. Tom provides no perfect example of Christlike living. Those who seek the flawless pastor to model after will have to look elsewhere. Does this make him a hypocrite? Tom doesn't think so. Hypocrisy is not failing to live up to what one preaches, but, rather, preaching what one does not believe. If our ideals and hopes are limited to our ability to demonstrate them, we will set our sights pretty low.

This means that Tom himself must decide whom to visit, what to preach, when to stay home with his family, and what he needs to do to take care of himself. No one else can direct his ministry. God gave Tom's ministry to Tom. This is true of all of us. We decide. Then we stand responsible to God for our choices.

When David grasps the truth of Tom's responsibility to make his own choices, David will benefit in two ways. He will not suffer from unfulfilled expectations of Tom, and he can forgive Tom's human mistakes.

Also, he can better appreciate why Tom must set his own priorities.

2. *The minister sets priorities.*

Sometimes Tom struggles with overload and feels he must quit or rupture. He has to make choices. It's simple. Since he can't do everything, he has the privilege of choosing what he will do. Many legitimate needs require an investment by Tom. He feels the pressure of others' expectations as well as of his own conscience. Yet he cannot fulfill every need. He sets priorities, often unconsciously.

If we live by the rule of the squeaking wheel gets the oil, then the most urgent-sounding need gets first attention. The quieter demands often don't get done. Tom begins by making certain assessments about himself. His choices declare: "This is who I am, this is what I do well. This is what seems most needed at the moment I decide." Unless he is clear in his own goals and strengths, he becomes like the cowboy who "jumped on his horse and rode off in all directions."

One of Tom's priorities is *preaching*. He will let few things rob him of the time he needs to prepare for preaching. When Tom multiplies the number of persons in the congregation on Sunday morning by the investment of time they each spend in listening to what he has to say, he feels a tremendous obligation to respect their trust. He owes it to them to be Biblical and fresh. Tom considers preaching his greatest opportunity to communicate the good news. This privilege excites him. He has made a personal vow never to enter the pulpit unprepared.

Another priority is *visitation*. He makes himself available to those who are in distress. Then, to those whom he wants to know and love better. "Visitation is the backbone of the church's ministry," he often says. Of course, lay people visit too. But no one else will take the place of the pastor knocking on a door. This says, "I cared enough to come." It is difficult for Tom to feel that he really knows a family until he sees them in the context of their own home. They also have a right to know him as their pastor on a one-to-one basis on their own turf.

Tom also needs the opportunity to spend time in *counseling*. He provides a climate where people feel safe to talk about who they are and what they feel.

In addition, Tom spends time doing administrative work. He gets involved in denominational activities and community projects, but these fall far below his first three concerns. He devotes time to them as he can fit them in his schedule.

Yet, Tom needs someone to minister to him. Thank God for the music minister who understands a minister's priorities and seeks to support him or her as a person.

3. *The minister needs support.*

As much as any member of his congregation, Tom needs affirmation. He needs a church within the church to be priests to him; that is, to encourage and guide him. In other words, Tom needs to be loved.

In some ways, the church is like a bank. Neither can survive without trust. When depositors lose faith in the bank, they make a run on it. No bank could pay all its obligations if they were all called up at the same time. In the same way, people also deposit their trust in the church. At times they need services in return. Fortunately not everybody needs ministering at the same time.

Sometimes, however, pastors and lay leaders simply fail. Ministers either don't hear, or don't understand, or are too busy meeting the needs of others. When this happens, some people will lose faith in the church. If enough lose confidence and call in their accounts at the same time, the church, like the bank, fails.

For Tom to function as a good pastor, he needs the trust of his members even when he fails.

It is not enough for Tom to spend time on a happenstance basis with those who love him. It is important for him to make opportunities to visit with them. To be with friends is a privilege which Tom must protect. From time to time we must stop by a service station or our cars run out of gas. In the same way, Tom must visit those who provide emotional support to him or his engine will simply stop.

Tom needs meaningful relationships, not because he is selfish or weak but because he is human. Tom needs David's support and understanding and love.

Someone has justifiably asked, "Who pastors the pastor?" If David can, his ministry of music begins on the most harmonious chord available to him.

V So Are
Ministers of Music

David graduated with honors from one of the most respected music schools in America. He holds two degrees in music and works full time in a large suburban church. He conducts seven choirs and four instrumental groups. He gives individual voice lessons. He spends his day organizing, planning, visiting, and doing the hundred-a-day little odds-and-ends jobs that are necessary to have the impressive music program he desires for his church. David's title is Minister of Music.

Sally is also a minister of music. The fact that she backed into it makes it no less a call from God. Because of her lack of musical skills, Sally feels that she has very little to offer. She is wrong. A member of her choir said of her, "The thing about Sally is, her faith just seems to smile." Whether she recognizes it or not, Sally offers a ministry.

Sally also edits a small-town weekly newspaper. All day long she gathers news, interviews local celebrities, sells advertising, even does job printing. Yet one night a week she meets a dozen fellow church members for choir rehearsal.

Music was not a part of her formal education, but she sang in her college choir. Now she leads the choir in her church. She was asked to take it on a temporary basis. "For two or three months at the most," they said, "while the church looks for somebody." That was nine years ago.

Sometimes she gets hurt. Members of the congregation who

would never think of telling the pastor that the prayers are too long will jab Sally with criticism. "Do we have to sing the hymns so fast?"

Sally smiles. "I'm so sorry the hymns seemed too fast. I'll try to slow them down next time." As she speaks, she remembers those in the choir who said, "Please, let's not drag the hymns this morning, O.K.?"

She wants to cry. "Can't you bear with me? I'd like to please you all but I don't know how."

Even with more musical training, Sally would still be caught in the cross-pull of those who need to criticize. But Sally doesn't know that. She thinks that if she were a better musician, the congregation would appreciate her more. That's not true. David gets criticized too.

It would be easy for Sally to quit. She wouldn't miss the small amount of money she makes for directing the choir. But who could do any better for a church this size? Besides, Sally loves the people in the choir. Someone else may produce better music, but no one could care more.

It is inaccurate to refer to Sally as a mere choir director. To do so gives the impression that she simply provides music. She does work with music, just as the preacher works with words. But music, like words, constitutes a tool for communication and relationships. Music transmits a message. What a beautiful medium for the message; and what a special calling to be a minister of music.

Not many pastors have the chance that the minister of music has to spend as much time with the same small group. Sally's job blesses her with the built-in opportunity to form relationships in a working context. A minister of music who believes that the function of musical performance outweighs the responsibility to minister to people will not succeed in what matters most.

Another way of looking at Sally's work is to say that *who* she is is more important than *what* she does. She cannot divorce her personhood from her ministry. Her faith and her personal relationship with God will have more to do with her effectiveness as a minister of music than her knowledge of notes and rhythm.

Let's look at Marvin, another minister of music.

Marvin feels unfulfilled. After serving a church for ten years, he decided to return to school. Now he works toward a Ph.D. in musicology. "Bach," he says, "is the father of it all. I want to learn about the musical sources of his middle years."

How sad! He might find more help if he studied human relations or psychology or any subject related more to ministry than to music. He does not realize that we cannot express Christian faith simply by making music.

As much as we might like to think that music speaks for itself, it does not. The message of music is incarnate in the musician. *Music expresses the musician, not the other way around.* The faith of the singer gives soul to the song.

Music is lived, not merely performed. Music that does not tell the musician's story is sound without substance. The musician ministers when singing of personal God experiences. Thus, the director's primary function is to provide the context in which this can happen. It is not an easy job.

David, the full-time professional, met Sally, the part-time volunteer, at a workshop where he taught a class on conducting methods. After class Sally joined in an informal discussion group. They shared job frustrations.

Sally said: "I could do a better job if I just knew what was expected of me. I've been directing a choir but I don't have a clear idea of my job."

David replied: "I've struggled with the same problem, and I've worked out some perspectives on it for myself. It seems to me that traditional theology describes Christ as a prophet, priest, and king. Even though they're not unique to us, I feel these are good terms to use in describing the functions of a minister of music."

I. *Prophet*

A prophet teaches a truth beyond academics or information-giving. A prophet proclaims what we really are. The truth sets us free. The minister of music is just such a teacher.

The art of singing involves far more than producing vocal sounds. Singing is theological. God has given to human beings the ability to use tongue, teeth, lips, and palate to form consonant sounds. In short, we can pronounce words. We shade and color vocal utterances to make vowels. God provides us with a priceless gift of vocal expression far more refined and expressive than that of any other creature. The process of vocal training frees the singer to be known, to disclose himself or herself.

As children, our most effective learning technique is imitation. We learn by trying to do what others do. Unfortunately, in trying to sound like others, we are up against an unbeatable handicap. We cannot hear our own voices.

When we speak or sing, others hear sound waves transmitted through the air and striking their eardrums. We, of course, hear a bit of this. But what we hear of ourselves is muffled by bone, muscle, flesh, and all the other physical properties in the head. The inner ear picks up mostly internal vibrations. Consequently, we don't hear our own voices as they sound to others.

When we start as children to mimic the vocal noises of others, we begin pulling, pinching, and covering the natural voice in an effort to make it "sound right." This effort results in a sound wrong for us.

The "affected" sounds we produce are shallow; they are not really our natural sounds. The first task of a voice teacher is to inspire us to sing our best. By helping us relax our phony techniques, the natural sounds may be freed.

The voice teacher who fulfills this task is a prophet, proclaiming the worth of each singer's expressions of personhood. This can be a frightening experience. We hide behind the mask of our "affected voices." Only when we feel secure can we attempt to overcome our negative habits. Thus, if voice teachers are to help us vocally, they must first support us emotionally.

For instance, when David became the director of our choir, Lawrence was singing first tenor—falsetto. He was also shy, overweight, and hypercritical.

When David asked him to stay one night after choir rehearsal to work on a solo part, Lawrence agreed reluctantly. He had never sung a solo. Even if he had, it couldn't have been heard beyond the third row.

In three weeks David had Lawrence singing with a full body-supported tone. At the next rehearsal Lawrence began using his new voice. The sound overwhelmed the choir. They applauded.

The following Sunday, Lawrence sang the opening tenor solo of McFarland's "Ho, Everyone That Thirsteth." The congregation saw that Lawrence had experienced something miraculous. *He* had changed. A year later, Lawrence was still saying, "I never knew it was in me."

Not only has Lawrence's voice continued to mature, but he has shed fifty pounds of excess weight. The singing itself didn't bring about fat reduction. But because he received emotional support and affirmation, he depended less on food to satisfy his inner needs.

One choir director tapped one man, worked with him, encouraged him, and called forth what he could be. As a result, Lawrence became a new person.

"My goal is to enable every singer to have a Lawrence experience," David said.

II. *Priest*

The most important quality a minister of music can bring to the task is a love for people. The ability to accept others as they are and to listen to them as persons of worth composes their highest characteristics. On the other hand, the minister of music who equates the job with musical productions or manipulates others for achievement becomes a parasite on the church. Love and concern for people must come through for sacred music to have integrity. It is not enough for ministers of music to love their "pets." They must also strive to love those who are difficult to love.

Lawrence was David's miracle. Scott remains an unknown.

Scott, a high schooler, constantly played the clown. Even when the rehearsal called for serious concentration, Scott was pulling for attention. He teased the girls, whispered smart remarks under his breath, and always asked the question that had just been answered.

Somewhat small for a ninth-grader, Scott palled around with boys one or two years younger. In the youth lounge at the church one night, Scott sat on the floor and pulled the drapes in front of him. Only his legs stuck out. Instead of laughing, Cindy asked: "Scott, why don't you come out and be one of us? I'll bet we'd like you if you weren't so silly."

David waited to see what Scott would do. Cindy's seventh-grade sensitivity amazed him. She had cut right to the heart of Scott's clowning mask. Every boring joke and irritating jab was really his cry for help.

"Oh, shut up," said Scott, "and leave me alone."

Well, thought David, it's going to take a little more time. And patience. But someday Scott will come out from hiding. I hope we'll still love him. Maybe I'll get a chance to talk with him tomorrow after rehearsal.

Whether he chooses to or not, David gets involved in pastoral counseling. Most of his care for people is simply supportive. He listens when they cry. Yet sometimes his support becomes therapeutic. By sharing insights about human dynamics he helps others to make healthy choices for their lives. David considers this an opportunity for ministry, not a burden. Sometimes his therapy is informal, as with Margaret Ann.

Margaret Ann, a lonely person, recently joined the rapidly growing population of widowed women over fifty. The choir has become her family. It is the one area of church where she belongs. Attending rehearsal is no casual matter for Margaret Ann.

This morning Margaret Ann received a notice in the mail. Taxes were going up on her house. The rest of her day has been unusually gloomy. Then at the evening meal things get worse. "Mom," her teenage son says, "how could you have possibly forgotten about my trip tomorrow? I told you twice. It's hard to believe how much we depended on Dad to keep things together around here."

Margaret Ann does not cry openly, but her feelings whirl around inside like spawning fish. She feels like an utter failure. Her son is right. They really did depend on Dad. She feels so alone.

Later, when the choir gathers for rehearsal, Margaret Ann needs much more than to be shown which notes to sing. Perfunctorily she sings her part. Feeling that she offers so little to the choir, she wonders why she joined it in the first place.

One criticism, one harsh word aimed at Margaret Ann tonight and she will probably quit. She needs a priest—someone to care about her, to listen to her pain, and to accept her as she is. The last thing she wants is to be offered love on the condition that she performs well. She just can't live up to any more demands for improvement. She needs support.

Does this mean that the choir is to become a therapy group? Yes. In fact, not become, it already is. A sensitive minister of music will create an atmosphere in which *people are more important than performances.*

Tonight Margaret Ann is crying out for help! David, by his facial expression, or short chitchat conversation, or a hug, can say, "I care enough to listen to you." Later during coffee break or after rehearsal or sometime the next day, he may become a priest to Margaret Ann.

On the other hand, the perfectionist choir director is not likely to recognize Margaret Ann as a hurting person. He or she is too busy concentrating on what people will think about how the choir performs. The choir's performance may just be a mask. The director knows that as long as people hear only the product, they might not look close enough to see that he or she hurts, too. The director carries around those same feelings of guilt, failure, and loneliness that Margaret Ann brought to rehearsal.

David isn't as much a musical artist as he is a priest. He is sometimes called upon to share honestly his own feelings and failures. Most of all, he is called upon to listen.

Someone has said: "A pretty girl is one I notice. A charming girl is one who notices me." To be a priest, one must be charming. David shows interest in others, not requiring them to be interested in him.

III. *King*

The minister of music is also a king. In planning, David leads. In performance, he dictates. In rehearsal, he rules.

It is time to start rehearsal, but there is so much talking that David can't get anyone's attention. Sitting in the bass section, Wayne surveys the various conversations going on. The men are talking about the cost of gas for their cars. Four others in turn are telling when they last changed motor oil. The tenors laugh about some CB jargon. Another group discusses new fall fashions. Three women discuss their children's schedules and illnesses. Two sopranos talk about their Sunday school classes.

This has been going on for over ten minutes. David is obviously anxious about the amount of rehearsal time being wasted. As Wayne listens, he becomes irritated. Why don't they hush so we can start? he fumes inwardly. After all, that's why we are here. David is ready to start. Why do we have to be so rude?

The truth is, David is the only one in the room who can get things started. He must take charge, or he disregards the personhood of everyone present.

The choir remains one organization in the church that must be run by a dictator. The democratic process is too cumbersome to function during a rehearsal. Individuals cannot take a vote on which pitch they want to sing or what tempo they will follow. The director is boss.

David must have clearly in mind precisely how he wants the choir to sound and exactly how to achieve it. He need not apologize for taking charge of his choir's preparation and performance. Like the quarterback of a football team, he calls the plays.

Even if what he asks for is by some standards "wrong," it will be better to do it his way than to have the choir pulling in different directions. Nothing is more insecure than sitting in a choir when the director is unsure of his own leadership. Nothing is more frustrating than waiting for everyone to express an opinion before the director gets to the next task. No wonder Wayne is irritated.

David rules in other ways. Perhaps no one else in the church has as many pieces to put together as the minister of music. To organize and schedule one choir is an enormous job but to coordinate and schedule several choirs demands unlimited vision, some planning, and a bit of luck. It cannot be done by a committee. David is king.

Does this not mean that the roles of priest and king sometimes clash? Yes, it does. Thus, part of David's kingly function is to determine when one role, for a while, dominates the other. However, each role is essential. David is, at the same time, responsible to Wayne and to Margaret Ann.

The concern of this book is that the priestly role of the minister of music is often neglected. Therefore, to err in the direction of "priesting" would only serve as a needed corrective.

When David or Sally is not actually leading the choir, each is no longer set apart as prophet or king. The role is always that of a priest, offering listening support.

The job of minister of music is not easy. But blessed is the church and the choir that has one, striving to fulfill that glorious calling.

VI Organists
Are People, Too

"Carol, this is too much! You're the best organist I know, but how you thought you could get away with this, I'll never know."

Tears filled Carol's eyes. She struggled to find words to explain herself. Reverend Tom Walker waited, expecting her to launch out in aggressive defense, to explain her side of the matter. Instead, Carol said, in a voice sounding like a child's, "May I be excused?"

It's just as well, Tom thought. His own anger prevented his hearing anything she might say.

Later, as he reviewed the incident in his mind, Tom could hardly believe what had happened. The clock read eleven. It was time to begin the service, but the prelude had not yet been started. Tom always entered the sanctuary with the choir after the organ was playing. So he waited.

Suddenly an usher called him aside. "Tom," said Otis, "I don't know what's going on, but Carol is sitting at the organ, staring at the congregation. Do you suppose she is sick?"

As Tom approached Carol to ask her if she was all right, Carol spoke. "You tell those people to be quiet. I'm not going to play a note with them talking like this."

"Carol," Tom said, "I know it must be frustrating. And we will do something, perhaps run an announcement in the bulletin urging everyone to approach the service of worship with more reverence. But right now, we're five minutes late! Please start the music now and I'll bring in the choir."

"I won't do it," Carol said. "Either you quiet them down or get someone else to play."

Tom's patience began to wear thin. "If you won't play today, Carol, we won't be needing you next week either, or any other week for that matter." As Tom walked away, trying to avoid a scene before the entire congregation, he heard Carol start the prelude.

Tom really meant what he had said to Carol. In his fifteen years as a church pastor, she ranked as the best organist he had ever heard. A superb accompanist, she could play anything. Her hymn-playing usually moved with excitement. She helped the congregation sing well. Tom felt that only one criticism could be made of her performance as a musician. Sometimes her hymn tempos seemed too fast.

But in her relationships with people Carol left much to be desired. Members of the choir described her as a "dead fish." Her attitude toward the world seemed to say: if you want to do anything other than listen to me play the organ, then I have no need for you! Carol spent most of her early years sitting at a keyboard. She felt that her only value in life came from playing the organ. Her security lay in performance.

Carol is now caught in a trap. Her drive for perfection, which makes her a superb musician, is destroying her as a person. She seems to have no sensitivity to the feelings of others.

A year after the incident over the prelude, the relationship between Tom and Carol had deteriorated to the breaking point. Tom had asked Carol to play a hymn at a slower tempo during the second service. But instead of retarding the hymn tempo, Carol actually played it faster.

After church she announced to Tom: "I am the professional musician. Don't tell me how to play hymns!" Her voice rose. "I'm a professional, not a hired hand to do things your way."

Tom jabbed back. "You have the option of resigning now or having me recommend to the committee that they fire you!"

Carol resigned.

Both Tom and Carol were relieved. The hostility between them had become unbearable.

Neither of them would have thought it possible that two years later they would again be working together. Their love and respect for each other would be stronger than their hatred had ever been. But that's what happened.

Less than a year after the firing, Tom asked Carol to come back. What changed Tom's mind? Of all those who had applied for the organist's job, none could lead the congregation in worship and singing nearly as well as Carol. That, alone, would never have caused Tom to want her back. Something else, very powerful, changed their relationship. It happened at the annual choir retreat.

David, their choir director, informed Tom that, in spite of extensive efforts, he had been unable to find a competent accompanist for the choir's retreat. David wondered if it would be O.K. to ask Carol. Tom reluctantly agreed.

Part of the program each year at choir retreat was spent in small-group sharing. Tom and Carol found themselves in the same group.

After some "community building" activity, the group leader asked, "Share one thing about yourself that we need to know to understand you." No one spoke for a minute. Then, one by one, each member began to open up. Most members kept their remarks on a light and humorous level, but others shared real inner feelings.

Tom revealed something of his constant struggle with a fear of failure. All the "I have everything under control" image, he confessed, is a big cover-up.

Carol had never before heard a pastor confess his own human failings and she began to see Tom in a new way. He further admitted that he takes his family for granted, that he wishes he could change, and that he doesn't know whether he can or not.

When the session was over, Carol sought out Tom. "I had no idea," she said. "Can I talk to you?" She began to cry. "My marriage is not good," she said. "I am yelled at every day at home. My husband would kill me if he knew I was telling you these things, but I have to tell someone."

That night Tom and Carol shared many things. They became priests to each other.

For the next six months Carol set up regular counseling sessions with Tom at the church. During that time Tom learned to know Carol as a warm and sensitive person. He wept with her as she shared the pain of her own childhood and young girl mistakes. He rejoiced with her as she gradually began to see herself as a person of innate worth. No longer did she need to hide behind her professionalism.

Tom recognized Carol as having precisely the kind of faith, sensitivity, and character that he longed for in himself and in every member of his staff.

Much against the advice of "it'll never work" expressed by friends of them both, Tom asked Carol to come back on staff. They have served effectively together now for six years.

During that time Tom has made several important observations about organists in ministry.

1. Organists are people, too. Often the system is stacked against them.

In spite of having such an audible responsibility, Carol, herself, maintains an extremely low profile. The congregation seldom sees her. Her relationship to the church is based primarily upon what she does, not upon who she is.

Consequently, it is not unusual to hear of an organist suddenly being "fired." Almost anyone, including the pastor, the chairman of the music committee, or the board of deacons, even the choir director, can get an organist dismissed. Few in the congregation will have much more involvement than hearing that they have a new organist whom also they will seldom see. Since the organ still sounds the same, what difference does it make?

Granted, the church needs procedures to make a change when the occasion demands it. However, it is equally essential to protect the organist against thoughtless acts or emotional whims.

The church could offer a renewable contract, one provision giving the organist the right of appeal to the official board in case of grievance. In too many cases, those in power violate the personhood of organists without providing any channel of appeal.

Why not have the personnel committee set up an annual conference? They may ask, "How is it going?" At least this gives them an opportunity to know the organist as a person. Any affirmation or support they can give will help the organist to do a better job.

2. Most churches pay organists regrettably little for their services. When Carol deducted from her take-home pay her car expenses, the cost of her personal music, lunches, and baby-sitters, there was little left. Church organists have no union.

Most of us fail to consider the amount of time spent in practice by a good organist. One parishioner remarked: "Why, I thought she learned to play all those songs while in school. I didn't know she still had to practice!" Many organists spend as much as eight hours a week practicing for the Sunday service. Some even more.

3. Tom learned to appreciate Carol's time. It is customary to require the organist to sit through wedding rehearsals. Often they start late and drag on interminably. Tom learned to insist on starting the rehearsal promptly. Carol was asked to come in thirty minutes later, "when we are ready for her

part." Respect for time and abilities affirms the organist's personhood.

4. Expressions of appreciation, both publicly and personally, are essential for healthy relationships. After all, how Carol sees herself reflected in the eyes of others influences her own self-image. And how she sees herself determines her relationship to the entire church.

5. Organists are ministers, too. That observation applies to every staff member in the local church. These persons are not just secretaries, bookkeepers, or speech givers. They are people servers. This includes the organist.

Tom and Carol are still learning.

Shortly after Carol had begun work with Tom the first time, an excited young couple talked to her about wedding music. A few minutes later, they were seen rushing from the church building, the bride in tears.

That afternoon the bride's mother called Tom. "We want another organist. We will not have that woman play for our daughter's wedding!"

Ten minutes later Carol called: "You will probably hear from the couple that came to see me this morning. I think I upset them."

"What happened?" Tom asked.

"I told her that I would not play 'Here Comes the Bride,' " Carol said. "I don't care if it was played for her mother's wedding, it's not appropriate for a Christian marriage service. If they want to embarrass everyone with a carnival act, O.K., but I refuse to be a part of it."

Tom tried to explain that this was a poor time to try to teach music appreciation.

Carol would have nothing to do with it. "I have my standards and I won't compromise for anyone."

But if we are truly in ministry, people must be loved and respected, even those who don't share our musical standards. Carol may have been right in principle. It is sad that she did not have patience to earn the respect she deserved before demanding conformity. Her musical standards were honored at the price of alienation. Ministers must be slow to insist that others live by their standards.

No one can know what meaning others find in any experience. Because "Here Comes the Bride" had been played at her parents' wedding, it had special meaning to the young girl who came to Carol. That, in itself, could have offered more spiritual support to the bride than the most appropriate music in the world. Most of what is gained from an experience depends upon what is brought to it. Past experiences determine the taste and understanding of what's happening now.

Another caution in holding standards absolute is that church leaders themselves have a poor record of identifying the standards.

History records issues for which persons were not only put out of the church but in some cases even burned at the stake for supporting the "wrong" viewpoint. Just as often, another church insisted on an opposing position. Those of us in ministry have been guilty of defending standards, not because they are objective norms, but because they are ours.

Tom and Carol have learned that people are more important than principles. Of course, that's the point. The *person* of the organist is more important than the *performance* of the organist.

VII The Choir's Practice

David, the minister of music, concerns himself more with people than with productions. He firmly establishes this position at the first rehearsal of every new year.

This is a story about a first rehearsal aimed at putting persons and performances in perspective.

Lucy, a member of the choir, shared their experience. "Rather than sitting in sections for singing, the choir sat in a big circle. David welcomed us back from vacation and then took the time to have each of us say something about ourselves. That helped us to know one another better.

"He explained that our first responsibility was to become a fellowship. He said, 'It's important to take time to build a community.'

"After fifteen minutes of this kind of personal sharing, David said, 'I want us to try something new tonight and I want you to know why.' Listening to him calmly asking for us to be open to a new kind of grace, I found myself glad that we were not yet into the warm-up of vocalizing. I wanted to be known more as a person than as a voice. I felt pleased about what David was doing even though I recognized that some of my friends in the choir were a bit uncomfortable.

"David explained: 'It has taken me a long time, but I have come to realize that I can do a few things well. God has given to me some gifts and I guess, for the first time in my life, I am beginning to feel O.K. about myself as a person.'

"After pausing to allow that much to soak in, he continued: 'This hasn't come easy to me. I have been taught all my life that we should not feel good about ourselves. It was not Christian. I have been led to believe that my duty as a person was to concentrate on those things about me I did not like and to spend my energies trying to correct my faults. I even spoke negatively about myself. I felt duty-bound from time to time to discuss my faults.

" 'Of course,' he went on to say, 'I lied a bit. I never would tell you what I saw as my real faults. I kept those covered up by a smoke screen of lesser evils which I thought would not seem too bad to others. Well, recently I have come to believe that it is important to me as a person and to you as members of the choir for me to affirm within myself my own sense of self-worth.

" 'What I would like us to do now is to divide into pairs, preferably to have you choose someone you do not know very well. Find a private corner in the room. Then I want you to share with your partner three things about yourself that you like. You might begin by saying, "I thank God that I am . . . " and go on from there.'

"Well, this was new to me," Lucy continued. "I had never done anything like this before. Certainly, not in a choir rehearsal. Bob and I paired off. I was relieved. We have been friends for a long time. Maybe we cheated a bit but I felt 'safe' in sharing with him. I was more relieved when he offered to go first."

" 'Three things I like about myself? I guess,' he said, 'I like the new sense of excitement I have found in my teaching. I am able to instill enthusiasm in my students. I am a better teacher now than I used to be. You know this, for we have talked about it before.'

"Then Bob went on to share that he was pleased with

certain disciplines in his life. In general he just liked himself better. As I listened to him, I began to feel more at ease with him and with what we were doing. That safe feeling didn't happen a moment too soon either because then it was my turn.

"So I said three things I like about me. I thank God that I am beginning to be open to his love. I am excited about some new feelings that maybe God does love me, even the way I am. I guess I am beginning to experience grace for the first time. I like that in me. It lets me be less judgmental. You know what I mean? And from that point, I guess we got off the subject.

"Then David asked us to join in groups of four and for each of us to introduce our partners to the others. This became a demonstration of how well we had listened.

"After only a few minutes for this, we assembled again in a large circle. David asked, 'What theological significance do you see in what we have just done?'

"I was surprised to see the group so responsive and willing to talk. Immediately one of the basses said, 'It says to me that what God has created is good, even if it's us!'

"Another said he realized that he was responsible to use his gifts for the glory of God and not just for himself.

"I said that to me the greatest issue was that of trust. I felt terribly vulnerable when I was saying that I liked something about myself. If Bob had flinched in any way, I would have been embarrassed and clammed up—forever! But I experienced his acceptance. That was valuable to me.

"David next asked, 'What does this have to say to us as a choir?'

"We spent the entire first rehearsal in building our choir into a close, supportive fellowship," said Lucy. "It was wonderful."

David believes that these sessions reveal some implications that are relevant to the ministry of music. The most important is that what we are is essential to what we do.

Only as we see ourselves as persons of worth can we affirm the worthfulness of others. Lucy explained. "As long as I live in fear of being exposed—in fear that you may see the real me that I think is bad, then we have no chance for fellowship. Most of my life I lived behind the mask, surprised somewhat at my performing abilities but afraid that you might see that I'm really not as good as I want to seem. I lived constantly on the defensive. Criticism simply destroyed me. I always had to be certain to show that it was 'unfair criticism.' As long as I saw myself as one who 'performs,' then every other member of the choir was a competitor. However, once I had enough faith and support in fellowship to affirm my own inner self-worth, then I no longer feared and judged you as a capable person. I am free to enjoy and celebrate us both."

Does this mean that how we, as a choir, perform is of no importance; that it makes no difference how we sound? Of course not. We still offer to God and to one another our most creative worship and service. But it says two things about our performance.

1. It says *we can perform better because we have experienced as well as proclaimed the gospel of grace and acceptance.* Members of a choir who love and care for one another are free to express their own being. The choir that professionally produces expressions of experiences that are foreign to them as a group merely performs. It becomes no more than a good "act." On the other hand, the church choir that becomes an example of its message has something genuine to sing.

2. *Performance is primarily for those who do it and not for those who hear it.* Those who are most involved in any activity stand to gain the most from it. The primary purpose of the choir is for the spiritual growth of those who participate in it. Jesus was very clear in saying that persons are more important because of who they are than for what they do.

We sing to the glory of God but that "glory" is not

something external. Our growth, faith, love, and fellowship are what truly glorifies God. Thus if tensions arise between excellence of performance and affirmation of persons, Jesus would opt for persons.

Come back, now, to David's question, "What does the affirmation of personhood have to do with us as a choir?"

One of the sharpest members of David's choir is Wayne. He spoke up. "I don't know if I can express this or not, but I feel that my voice is one of the most personal things about me. Most of us are not so self-conscious about our hands or elbows as we are about the sound of our own voice."

Wayne continued. "At least if we are self-conscious about our hands, we can keep them in our pockets. The only way to hide our voice is to mumble. Many of us are anxious about singing or public speaking because we feel so exposed.

"If I understand vocal physiology rightly, the primary function of the larynx is not to make vocal sounds, but to keep food from entering the windpipe when we swallow. Also, the larynx closes off oxygen to increase our strength when we suddenly strain or grunt. If that's the case, then our vocal cords are primarily defensive in nature. That means to use them to express ourselves rather than to defend us, we must feel safe."

Guy, one of the tenors, asked Wayne, "Do you mean I have to feel comfortable with you guys to sing well?"

"That's precisely what I mean," said Wayne. "My feeling of self-worth is directly related to my ability to perform. I believe stage fright, the subject of much psychological study, is in direct proportion to the degree that I feel I must impress you with my performance to be recognized as a person of worth."

By this time David was beginning to feel some time pressure, for he had spent more than the rehearsal hour enabling his choir members to get to know one another and develop an appreciation for the unique worth each brought to the group. Without exception, though, the entire choir thought this was a significant way to start the new year—together.

Later, reflecting on what had happened, Lucy thought maybe this was related to what Jesus meant when he scolded the Pharisee for cleaning the outside of the cup when the inside was unattended.

"Maybe if we are to be an effective group in the ministry of music, we cannot concentrate all our energies on polishing up what shows just on the outside," she said. "At least, for me, I know I would have to start with my own inner self-image. I thank the Lord for giving me a group of supportive friends with whom I can grow and express my faith."

VIII   Notes
to Harmonize Discord

David had no chance of accomplishing his hopes when he introduced the new anthem. But he didn't know that.

He was aware of only the reasons for his own enthusiasm. The text expressed an affirmation of God's love for his people. The music was fresh and dramatic.

Just last week the choir had defined its purpose as being a supportive fellowship. The members recognized the importance of affirming one another.

David knew the choir would sing the new anthem better if he gave the members the opportunity to discuss its value and relevance before rehearsing it. He believed that the discussion would be another mountaintop experience.

It was not. David had no way of knowing how many hidden agendas, both consciously and subconsciously, were at work.

Meet some of the members of the choir and their agendas:

BERT   is a banker. By nature he is used to making decisions quickly, without having them challenged. But tonight, just before coming to choir rehearsal, Bert's wife had challenged a decision he had made. In fact, an emotional explosion had occurred. Her last words to him were: "O.K., you go on to choir, but when the Smiths get here, don't expect me to entertain them by myself. They are your friends, too. You had better get home early." Bert certainly had no control over when out-of-town friends would suddenly drop in. He was already feeling the pressure to get back home. Maybe he should have skipped choir tonight.

CHERYL   is an attractive blond soprano soloist. Her mother-in-law will be visiting them next month. But on that day, David has chosen for them to sing "God Loves Everybody," which has an alto solo. She is not a pushy type of soprano, but if the anthem has not already been selected . . . , it sure would be nice to have the choir sing "Behold, What Manner of Love." It is romantic in style and would give her an opportunity to do the solo. She is wondering, Could I get David to change his mind?

VIRGINIA   was recently elected an elder, one of the first women to have this opportunity in their church. Virginia has not experienced what being an elder involves, but she is sure that she represents the "official vote" in the choir. She enjoys the feeling of authority.

BILL   is usually easygoing, and agreeable. However, right now Bill has a problem. His business is in a financial bind. As much as he hates to "impose on a church relationship," Bill knows that next week he will be calling on Bert at the bank to request a loan. Bill perhaps is unaware of it himself, but tonight he will do anything to attract Bert's favor. Whatever Bert says tonight, Bill will support.

WAYNE   sees himself as the backbone of the choir. He has the strongest voice and has studied vocal methods. He feels somewhat like the "daddy" of the choir and will want to help David do the best job he can. However, Wayne gets annoyed when the choir gets a little out of control.

PERRY   is usually quiet. However, his wife recently lost the elder election to Virginia. Perry is trying to deal with his feelings on this, but every time Virginia comes out with her authoritarian tone, Perry can't help challenging it.

These are some of the hidden agendas which members of the choir brought to rehearsal tonight. Everyone, including David, had something going on inside in addition to preparing to lead in worship.

Hidden agendas are inevitable. We have passions and responsibilities that cannot be left behind because we give our time for choir rehearsal. In addition to other loyalties, we have numerous personality needs and goals that become a part of all that we do.

Every choir, because it is made up of people working together, operates as a small group.

The exciting beauty of the music ministry is that the choir director has the unique privilege of working with this small group for an hour or more every week. Relationships of esteem develop in small groups far beyond anything possible in larger, more formal settings. For years, social scientists and church leaders have been affirming small groups as an authentic expression of the church's message.

We are all born with certain basic needs. We require food, shelter, and warmth to stay alive. In order to avoid being overwhelmed by anxiety, we must also achieve some measure of security and stability. When these basics are met, other needs surface, calling to be satisfied. We yearn for social and emotional self-fulfillment. These can best be fulfilled in a group. Hidden beneath the surface of most of us is the need for belonging, acceptance, self-expression, and productivity. These are not selfish but normal.

Everybody needs to stand high in the eyes of others. We want respect and appreciation. We all crave esteem.

Esteem is not the same as status. We get status if we inherit a lot of money, no matter what kind of person we are. Status may be granted out of fear. On the other hand, esteem is always a gift from those who respect us. This good self-image is not only important for our emotional health, but it forms the root of our relationship with God. He accepts us. We are his children. That's great news!

Yet self-esteem does not come easy. Many of us have been programmed negatively. Ten friends may share their honest appreciation for David as a person, but if only one person points out a fault, all the positives are wiped out. We are told that all these "not O.K." feelings really began in childhood when we were offered a conditional love, the kind of love you get only when you are good or quiet, or "perform right."

To correct this condition is precisely the opportunity of the choir—to offer the gospel's affirmation to each of its members. In fact, *unless the choir seeks to practice the gospel's acceptance with its members, it has no honest message to sing to the church.* In spite of the quality of its tone, without love, its message is hollow hearsay.

David has been studying the characteristics common to small groups and relating them to the choir. He found that every small group interacts on two levels and that the effectiveness of the group is directly related to its cohesion. By his awareness of these characteristics, David has been ministering to the choir in ways that recognize these factors.

I. *Every choir operates on at least two levels.*

The first and most obvious level on which the choir operates is task accomplishment. The job of the choir is to perform. The members work hard toward this end.

Each member performs. The contribution of each is measured and judged. Individual value is determined by talents.

Every choir director works diligently on this surface level. Schools engaged in training choir directors stress production. Some choir directors, aware of nothing but this level, have the choir's performance as their only interest.

A second set of dynamics, however, operates at the same time. Called the process level, it involves individual psychological needs. Every group contains a hidden world of emotional life.

In fact, social and emotional needs motivate persons to join the choir. They come in with the basic question, How do I relate as a human being to these other persons? Choir members socialize, consciously or unconsciously. Friendships form. The need for belonging is fulfilled.

Along with these social needs, other unknown forces block wholehearted participation. As David learned, the most significant are the *hidden agendas.* An alert choir director is aware that no matter what the publicly agreed task, something else is always going on under the table. These hidden, undisclosed needs siphon off energy necessary for the choir to accomplish its task. When this happens, choir members do not work logically or respond intelligently. They are sluggish, and often wrangle over unimportant points while missing the main thrust. Before choir directors become too disciplinary, they need to remember that choirs work simultaneously on both levels. Only one is formally announced. The other is unlabeled and covert. Yet it is deeply felt and involves emotional conflicts and scores of psychological forces. Such is the case with Jack.

While rehearsing a section of *The Crucifixion,* Jack took every opportunity to talk to the other tenors. He reexplained

David's instructions and even told jokes. The music was somber but Jack just couldn't get in the mood. David was annoyed. Only later, when Jack recalled his irrational behavior could he associate this singing of *The Crucifixion* with their rehearsal of it two years ago. At that time, Jack's father was in the hospital. Now, subconsciously, he was aware that the sounds, sights, and even the weather were the same as they had been when his dad died. Jack covered up his unrecognized anxiety with jokes.

1. Hidden agendas are most obvious *when the group is faced with a crisis*. The choir tends to fall apart. When the rewards of togetherness are endangered, individuals operate out of private goals. When threatened, most of us will become defensive. Hidden agendas have to be cleared out of the way before the choir can get on with its task. Any effort to bury or ignore them blocks both process and task achievement.

The alert choir director listens for hidden agendas and learns to recognize signs of their presence. A good question to ask in trying to uncover hidden agendas is, "Have we said all that we feel about this matter?" Given a chance, locked-in concerns will surface. On the other hand, to criticize a group or individual for the presence of hidden agendas not only is unfair but produces negative results.

Jack did not really know why he was being disruptive. Had David scolded him as some choir directors are prone to do, nothing would have been gained. Jack would have been embarrassed and David, angry.

Probably there was no way for David to help Jack unpack his feeling during the rehearsal. David could call for Jack's attention, but his tone of voice and how he looks as he speaks communicates either affection or rejection. To recognize Jack's needs for support is the beginning of being his priest. Possibly later, during private time, David could be a caring listener. But what can he do to lessen interference while it is going on?

During one rehearsal David led an open discussion on the subject of hidden agendas. He wanted to help the choir mature in dealing with both levels of its process. When hidden agendas were recognized and openly talked about, they were easier to handle.

David warned the choir members, however, that some things may be personal and could hurt by exposure. No one should ever disclose to a choir information that would make anyone look bad.

David tries to be sensitive to every person's needs. He knows that the more acceptance and trust a choir member feels, the less the destructive forces take over.

He keeps two things in mind. First, helping another to deal with a harmful hidden agenda may be more ministry than the best music one can produce. Second, he has learned that he, too, is susceptible to agendas that create ambivalence and tension within himself.

2. Another factor relating to hidden agendas is *divided loyalties.* David understands that the members belong to more than one group. In addition to being members of a choir, they bring to rehearsal with them loyalties to their family, community, profession, social organization, and political party. This can lead to confusion and high levels of stress.

Ramon wants to welcome Mary into the church and into the choir. She has a beautiful soprano voice. But Mary is black. Ramon also belongs to the real estate board and he is concerned about the effects on property values if Mary and other blacks move into the community.

All divided loyalties are not so dynamic. Jackie is simply caught in a meeting conflict between the choir and the planning committee of the PTA. She wants to be present in both places. Emotionally, she will be.

The sensitive choir director is aware of the tensions the members of the choir feel because of their devotion to other legitimate groups. To demand single allegiance is unrealistic.

Most members of the choir can give a high level of attention during rehearsals and want to do so. Else they would not be present. For the director to be understanding when other loyalties cause preoccupation shows a respect for the personhood of choir members. It also leads to greater loyalties over the long haul. An appreciated member of any group has more desire to be a loyal member.

Just as David understands how the hidden emotional needs of members affect the group, he also works with another principle:

II. *Every choir's effectiveness is directly related to its cohesion.*

Cohesion binds the choir together. Cohesion is the feeling of closeness, warmth, self-esteem, importance of one's contribution, and the overall feeling of belonging. The significance of this element for the choir cannot be overstated.

The cohesive choir works better. Members help one another and are less competitive because of their team spirit. The choir becomes an expression of the message it sings.

We of the church are committed to the principle that people are more important than production. We have a mandate to love our fellow human beings. We are called to appreciate the value of one another. David recognizes that every member of his choir needs recognition and praise. The choir that affirms its members becomes more effective in communicating the good news.

David has learned several ways to contribute to greater morale:

1. He often mentions the choir as a group; talks about *our* choir and the things for which *we* stand. He does not accentuate the "I" or lead by saying, "I want from *my* altos thus and so," or "I expect you to do this for *me*." The choir belongs to itself.

2. He stresses teamwork. He lifts out past accomplishments. He often talks about the choir's history, builds

traditions, develops an image, even uses nicknames, to create the feeling of belonging together.

3. He avoids falling into the trap of preoccupation with star members. The quiet, less talented members also need affirmation. The member who says, "I don't care if I have the solo or not, let's just do our best as a choir," is a great booster of the choir's esprit de corps. David tries to set the groundwork where this can happen.

4. Contribution to the choir's cohesion involves rewards. David has in mind dinners and social gatherings. He also offers intrinsic rewards, such as being prepared for rehearsals. He sees that the room and materials are ready. He comes on time. He recognizes a job well done, expresses appreciation for faithfulness, and treats choir members like people, not machines. After a good service of worship, he often says, "It couldn't have been done without each one of you."

Here are a few more suggestions of how cohesion is increased:

1. Again, the minister of music needs to listen. Social scientists tell us that most people in our society have a great need simply to have someone listen to them. Many dehumanizing forces cause us to feel lost. To have someone really pay attention to us, no matter what we say, is an affirming experience.

Listening is ministry. Yet many in ministry, whether preaching or music, have been trained "to tell." We get so locked into the syndrome of getting across our information that sometimes we overlook the importance of allowing others to get across their information.

It takes a positive effort to listen. Choir directors who take time to ask, "What has happened to you lately?" and then listen, will be surprised how much those quiet people have to say. They will also become aware of a closer, more trusting bond of friendship among members of the choir. An affirmed member affirms others. The person who feels unaccepted becomes critical and suspicious.

Listening involves responding not to words only but to feelings. It is worthwhile to ask oneself when another is talking, especially in a crisis situation, What is going on in him that makes him say that? Too often, when another is talking, we already have our minds preoccupied with what we are going to say back.

Persons who grow in ministry find they talk less, listen more, and listen most to feelings.

2. In any communication, there is both a "sender" and a "receiver." The sender is always giving information about the sender. Even if her words sound judgmental, she only reveals information about herself, the sender. To say, "I hate your choice of music for this service," says less about the chooser of music than about the one who is talking. Choir directors who realize this will find themselves being less defensive and more able to understand what is really going on. They can then offer greater support.

3. Criticism encourages defensiveness; it seldom helps another to grow. The only person David can really change is himself. Choir directors who set out to improve others head toward defeat.

They may encourage others to grow only by offering support. It does little good to give pep talks, threaten, beg, or even cry if it is done to coerce. More important is the goodwill we feel for those with whom we work. Often, what we label as apathy is no more than our own failure to provide a structure where members of the choir have their emotional and social needs met.

Cohesion within the choir will result in the kind of Christian witness that proclaims God's love both *to* and *through* the ministry of music.

Several years ago a black family joined Tom and David's all-white congregation. Fourteen white families quietly dropped out. Members became anxious. A few even questioned, "Will our church fall apart?" Some became suspicious of Tom and questioned his leadership.

Members of the governing board criticized one another. They hardly knew one another, because church officers met together once a month and served only three-year terms before rotating off. They ruled the church but had very little shared history.

The same was true in the Sunday school. Teachers worked in separate rooms and rarely assembled for fellowship. No wonder the church felt threatened. Morale was on the bottom.

The cohesion of the choir was the glue that held the church together. One member said: "I'm not sure I like what's going on, but I've been a part of this church for a long time. I'm not about to give it up now." Not one choir member left.

Tom quickly recognized that the presence of the choir in full attendance each Sunday had a calming effect on the congregation. The *choir's practice,* that is, the love of its members for one another and for their church, became the example that led their congregation through a time of crisis.

IX The Church
Is Always Saints

Tom Walker and David Bailey not only work for the church, they are the church. They are in it together and neither can be the church without the other. This coincides with their view of the church as primarily a fellowship of God's people. Thus their relationship to each other is not only personal but also theological.

Tom and David walked through the new sanctuary late one afternoon. The sun shone softly through the stained-glass windows. A mystical hue filled the room, adding to the sense of majestic loftiness created by a high ceiling and exposed beams. Remembering how hard they both had worked to see this sanctuary dream come true, David said: "I know, Tom, they say it's a sin to be proud. But when you stand here in the sheer beauty of this place, you must feel at least a bit . . . satisfied."

Tom demurred: "No, it's not a matter of pride. I guess I am satisfied."

Later, however, when he compared what happens here to what is going on in other churches of equal size, Tom admitted that he really felt proud.

At the same time he couldn't enjoy the success. The many people whom the church failed to reach and challenge robbed him of satisfaction. He thought also of those not involved in the program of Christian education, the token givers, those

who come only at Easter and Christmas, and those on the
inactive rolls. The church had grown. But slowly. Almost as
many old members moved away as new ones joined. But the
church was growing, and Tom was proud.

On the other hand, Tom thought of the early church in the
book of The Acts. Those early Christians had no new
building, no full-scale programs. Yet five thousand joined
their fellowship in one week. Tom asked David: "Why did
those folks do that? What did they find to make them want to
belong? And what did those early preachers tell them? Jesus
saves? That in itself wouldn't have done it.

"They would have said, 'Saves from what?' From hell?
They didn't preach any impassioned message about suffering
eternal damnation. That's our game. We are the ones who try
to 'scare the hell out of people,' to get them to come. The first
Christians knew what 'hell' was. They had experienced it.
John the Baptist had been beheaded; the disciples, executed.
They could hear the shrieks of agony of those who were
persecuted because they had opposed Rome. When they
joined the church, they didn't escape torment. They ran the
risk of it. So, why in the world did they come?"

Tom used to think people joined the church in order to join
God. It was a necessary step in being reborn. That's partially
true when it leads to the experience of being the people of
God. It is not simply a legal requirement. Tom knows now that
if people were not already united to God, they would have no
interest in the church. They join the church to *join us.*

Tom also used to think that "church" was what preachers
did up front. Ministers controlled the grace. By preaching the
Word and rightly administering the sacraments, they dis-
pensed grace to those who came to get it. Week after week
Tom worked hard to be sure that the sermon and the anthem
were of good quality so that his people would be sure to come
back to church for more.

And theology was something he found in books. Every

week he would dust off a few, read until he found some concept about God that seemed fresh, then he would stand before a congregation and explain it to them. Afterward he would put the book back on the shelf until it was needed again.

Tom knows better now. Real theology, the real church, and the living Christ is that which is in each of us.

Tom once said: "You don't come to church to meet Christ. You bring him here with you. You don't just come to worship. Your coming is worship."

The Christ we know is the Christ revealed in persons. John Calvin said that the Scriptures are the spectacles through which we can see God. Tom prefers to think of faith as the spectacles through which we can see life with the eyes of one who believes in God. We look through the eyes of faith to see the world as God intended it to be, to see one another as God intended us to be. Faith allows us to see God in the world and in one another. *Christ is in us and we are the church—together.*

The big word is *together.* Being the church means being united. We don't come to worship alone looking only for God. We come to worship because others are here. We need their presence. None of us has faith enough to sustain it alone.

There is no way to understand what the church is without an appreciation of the word "together." Tom searched all his ministry for the right word to express the concept of the church as our life of faith together.

The church is a community, but it is more. Community has limitations. It suggests task and turf. Tom is trying to describe something more than where we live and what we do.

One word for "community in a special sense" is a Greek word, *koinōnia.* This powerful word for the church is found in the New Testament some twenty times. *Koinōnia* stands at the very heart of the church. It means fellowship. Yet this word also has its limitations. It has great meaning but it has also become vague by overuse.

Tom has chosen the word *communitas* to describe the

church. *Communitas* is the Latin word for community, but Tom likes it because it does not carry with it the limitation associated with the English word. *Communitas* is precisely the *koinōnia* described by Luke in the book of The Acts.

> They met constantly to hear the apostles teach, and to share the common life, to break bread, and to pray. A sense of awe was everywhere, and many marvels and signs were brought about through the apostles. All whose faith had drawn them together held everything in common: they would sell their property and possessions and make a general distribution as the need of each required. With one mind they kept up their daily attendance at the temple, and, breaking bread in private houses, shared their meals with unaffected joy, as they praised God and enjoyed the favour of the whole people. And day by day the Lord added to their number those whom he was saving.
>
> The whole body of believers was united in heart and soul. Not a man of them claimed any of his possessions as his own, but everything was held in common, while the apostles bore witness with great power to the resurrection of the Lord Jesus. They were all held in high esteem; for they had never a needy person among them, because all who had property in land or houses sold it, brought the proceeds of the sale, and laid the money at the feet of the apostles; it was then distributed to any who stood in need. (Acts 2:42-47; 4:32-35, NEB)

The whole body of believers was *united in heart and soul.* They were all *held in high esteem.*

They had *never a needy person among them*. ("Needy" was as much defined in terms of loneliness, anxiety, and frustration, as by hunger.)
They *shared their meals with unaffected joy*.
They *praised* God.
They *studied* the apostles' teachings.
And, they *enjoyed the favour* of the whole people.

Does anybody in today's world need that? No wonder five thousand joined them in one day. Their church was respected, honored, feared, and slandered, but never ignored. Even pagans described them by saying, "How those Christians love one another!" We are stirred when we realize what the church was meant to be. We also become a little ashamed. How far we are today from Christ's intention for the church! Masses joined the apostles' church because they experienced forgiveness, acceptance, and love.

Tom believes that the church today is facing a crisis of membership because it lacks *communitas*.

> Someone defined the crisis in other ways, saying:
> The church is a busy and boring luxury cruise ship, whose passengers are absorbed by status and self-interest, while the ocean around is filled with helpless humanity clinging to drowning wreckage.
> (June Callwood, *Why the Sea Is Boiling Hot,* p. 19; Toronto: Ryerson Press, 1965)

This description of the church may be justified. We need critics to make us aware of human suffering, to quicken our sense of mission.

However, another crisis lays a prior claim upon us: the lack of community *(communitas)* within the church. *We can only be to the world what we are first to one another*.

Folk art has pointed out that when wolves attack the wild

donkeys of the Great Northwest, the donkeys circle in, put their heads together, and kick outward until the wolves are either driven off or kicked to death. In the church it is just the opposite. When the wolves attack us, we do not put our heads together and kick outward. We kick one another to death—and wonder why the wolves win!

So what about the *communitas* in The Acts? Is the life-style of that early church an impractical ideal? Is the picture of Christians who genuinely love, accept, and serve one another merely a charade perpetuated on the innocent and the unsuspecting? Is Luke just telling us the earliest church joke? Let us hope not. Maybe God makes this kind of loving fellowship possible and we have failed to tell the good news of it with convincing clarity.

Two little girls talked about the Christmas pageant. The first said, "Wasn't the baby Jesus the sweetest thing in the world?"

Her young friend answered, "Yes, but it's a shame he had to die."

"No problem," said the first. "After three days, he rose from the dead and lived happily ever after."

"No kidding? Nobody told me that. And that's the very best part!"

Maybe that's the way with the church, too. We fail to tell the very best part. The church first existed as a loving fellowship where followers of Christ worshiped God and cared for one another.

At times in his own church life Tom has also experienced *communitas*. He relates his experience on a choir retreat. "We worked, planned, and prayed together. We spent time playing and laughing. Late on the last night, we shared in a Communion service.

"Afterward someone said to me: 'Say, this was great. Why can't we keep this spirit and carry it back to our church?'

"I tried to analyze what had happened," Tom said. "I knew

we all felt very close and loving. I wanted to carry that back, to reproduce it for the whole congregation. But it never worked.

"But no wonder we could never reproduce *communitas,* for we had not produced it in the first place. When *communitas* happens, it's always a gift. It's a here-and-there, now-and-then happening. At best we can only recognize it and celebrate it together."

Furthermore, *communitas* never happens when we are performing our job roles. It is not when one is Tom, preacher, and another is Joe, layman, or Sally, singer. On the contrary, it is when our roles peel away and we are just people in Christ that it happens.

For this reason, Tom and David call each other by their first names. They also call members of the congregation by their first names. The church is a family. Members of the same family belong together and do not address one another as Mister, or Doctor, or Miss. It was a little uncomfortable at first, but soon even the older members appreciated being included on a first-name basis.

Before the service each Sunday, Tom stands out in front of the church greeting people as they come in to worship. He tries to call each person by name. Tom dresses in a business suit rather than a robe so that he will not contribute to the feeling of separation between clergy and laity.

The choir share a unique fellowship. Even as they come together at 10:40 A.M. to practice for the eleven o'clock service, they enjoy a special feeling toward one another.

"Good morning, Mary. I hear your Susie was sick Friday," a friend says.

"Oh, yes, but she is better now, thank you."

Even such a small exchange shows belonging and concern. In the choir, anyone absent is missed.

David works hard to enable the choir to perform its best during the service of worship. At the same time, he is grateful for every happening of *communitas.*

When the service begins, Carol plays two preludes. As soon as the first prelude begins, Tom goes into the sanctuary and *sits with the congregation.* This short, silent time of preparation enables Tom to be identified as coming to worship with the common flock of God's people and not as one set above.

Following the first prelude, announcements welcome the congregation and share the concerns of the church. During this time the congregation is invited to stand and welcome one another to the house of the Lord. "Tell them your name," Tom urges. "If you don't know their names, chances are they don't know yours either."

From time to time the choir waits until the congregation is greeting one another before entering the sanctuary. Walking in from the back, choir members come down the aisle speaking to members of the congregation. Gradually they make their way to the choir loft.

Meanwhile Tom steps into the wing and puts on his pulpit robe. The beginning of the second prelude calls the congregation to order and the service of worship begins.

Communitas happens in a warm church where friends are recognized and welcomed. Worship for Tom and David includes belonging to a caring family.

Communitas does not come easy and not everyone wants it. Sometimes it is hard to love and accept others. However, the message of the pulpit and the choir loft is always the same: God's unconditional love. As we gradually realize that God cares for us, we develop a life-style of caring for one another.

When Tom speaks of the church as *communitas,* he is not talking about some shallow Pollyanna "I'm O.K., you're O.K." "I need you with me precisely when I am not O.K.," he says. "When I am hurting so bad that when you come close to me, I may clobber you."

Communitas is costly; it involves bearing crosses. It is not easy to love those who behave unlovingly. Christian love is best revealed by a cross.

When Harold tried out for the Christmas pageant, he wanted to play the part of Joseph. Instead he was selected to be "just a shepherd." Further evidence of miscasting came when his sister was chosen to play an angel. During the rehearsal, the teacher directing the pageant marked an "X" on the stage floor to show each character where to stand. Harold knew his spot very well.

On the afternoon of the pageant, Harold was dressed in his robe and slippers in ten minutes, while it took his sister all afternoon to get on her big white dress with hoops, wire up her halo, and adjust her wings. By curtain time, Harold was thoroughly disgusted.

In great splendor, the angels took their places. The director's only oversight was a failure to realize that the hoops in the angels' dresses caused them to spread out and completely cover some of the "X's." When Harold entered, he couldn't find his spot. He approached his "X" from one direction, then another. Finally he pranced full circle, walked to center stage, waved his arms as though to lead a mass gathering in prayer, and said loudly: "Now what do I do? The dumb angels have covered up all the crosses!"

The gospel makes no effort to cover up the crosses.

Yet we do not take up a cross to buy God's love. We take up our cross of discipleship to make our relationship with him and his people more real.

We take up our cross in caring for one another. One such act of caring involved a medical missionary serving in Egypt. He was distressed that the people he loved and served were suffering from a strange anemia. It was widespread and life-strangling. Efforts to treat their affliction by medicine proved useless. Finally, he learned that the disease was caused by a liver fluke found in the soil of the riverbank. After isolating a disease-producing sample, he returned to

America, to Johns Hopkins Medical School, where research could be done to seek a cure and save his people. But immigration authorities stopped him. "Under no circumstances are you going to bring diseased liver flukes into this country."

He pleaded, but to no avail. He would have to dispose of the flukes before he could come into the country. He walked down the hall of the men's room, stood in front of the lavatory, took the top off the jar, and was about to empty its contents down the drain.

Suddenly he remembered his friends in Egypt. Without hesitation he lifted the vial to his lips and swallowed its contents.

The next five years of his life were spent struggling to stay alive. He was a long way from North Africa. Yet he was still in *communitas* with his friends.

In the New Testament, almost without exception, the word "saints," not "saint," is used.

We are always in it together. That's *communitas*. And that's what it means to be the church. More than anything else, Tom and David work for this oneness together. If it means personal sacrifices or special efforts to affirm each other, those on a church staff have a unique calling to serve as a team. Their working together produces more than better performance. They exhibit the nature of the church.

Postlude:
The Song We Sing

The song we sing is good. It is called grace.

I have often felt that if I just had five days, or even five hours in which I were free to listen, God would surely speak to me. It would have been important to me if he had done so. I would have listened and now I would have been able to say, "Hear the new word from God."

However, nothing like that has happened. I have had many hours free. God has had ample time to tell me anything he wants me to know. I have been more quiet than usual and God has been terribly silent.

This disappoints me. His silence has pushed me back to the old recourses of friends, books, and memories that have always sustained me. I won't give an authoritative new chapter but will reaffirm the same old word I have already said, done, thought, experienced, and half-believed all my life.

For the prophets, the only requirement for writing a book was to begin by saying, "Thus saith the Lord." Later the church fathers would write: "The church has always said. . . ." But the most I can say about the gospel we sing is, "It seems to me." I can't say, "Thus saith the Lord," because he doesn't always speak to me. Nor can I say, "The church has always said . . . ," for the church has seldom had enough unity to have always said anything. The most honest thing I can say is, "It seems to me."

So, it seems to me:

First, the major reason for a portion of the congregation to be separated into a choir is to proclaim the church's message of grace. There are many fringe benefits in having a choir in worship but the most legitimate purpose is to communicate the good news in other tones than those simply spoken.

John Calvin, the great Reformer, felt the purpose of the choir was to respond to the proclamation of the Word. Thus, his choir wound up in the balcony so that it would be inconspicuous. Its music and text were limited to praise. The influence of Calvin is still prominent among worship leaders and church architects even today.

It seems to me that the primary purpose of the choir is not response but "proclamation." If all the choir does is reply, then why not have the entire congregation respond? Why separate some according to talent? For response the number one choir is always the congregation. However, the choir exists so that those who have singing talent may proclaim the gospel in ways that are emotionally moving and dramatically clear.

For this reason, it seems to me that the choir should sit in the front of the sanctuary. God speaks through personalities. I can remember a choir director leading in prayer before each service of worship by saying, "Lord, make us invisible that this congregation might not see us but Christ." I appreciate his respect for the central place of Christ in worship, but I wish that instead he had prayed, "Lord, turn us on, that this congregation might see Christ in us." The hope of the church is not that we might see Christ "up there" or somewhere beyond but that we might learn to see Christ in one another. Facial expression, eyes, deportment, and symmetry of the choir communicate as much as the sum of its words.

Second, it seems to me that because of grace God is in mission. He is in history as a father looking for his straying children. He gives us a commission that we should also seek him—in one another. If I were God and I saw my children seeing Christ in one another, treating one another with the love and respect we would show to Christ, I don't think I would be sad. Christ in each of us is God's gift to all of us.

On the other hand, if status with God is something I have to achieve or if his presence in me must be earned, then I can't really love you. We are competitors. I will live defensively, for when I see your godliness I can never be sure I still measure up. Or worse, seeing your lack of faith, I will feel superior.

God's presence in all of us, known as the Holy Spirit, is the choir's most fundamental characteristic. Thus, the choir's keynote is its gracious treatment of each of its members as the dwelling place of God.

Ideas are great and most of us thrill to hear a new one. But ideas need to come down to a practical level. All our excitement about abstract theological concepts is to no avail unless we at least try to put them into practice where we live. The choir sings with integrity when it strives to practice the grace of God's acceptance which it proclaims.

The gospel declares good news to frightened, lonely people. I don't have to "scare" people to get them to come to church, to give their money, or to sing. The gospel declares that God wants our love, not our fear.

A little boy crawls up in his mother's lap with a windblown, bug-eaten flower he pulled up by the creek. "Mommy, I brought you this because I love you." What an exciting experience that is for the mother. How different it would be if the lad brought his gift and said, "Mommy, I knew you were gonna get me if I didn't bring you this gift."

Do we come to God and love him because we know he's going to punish if we don't? *Does God want anything less than love freely offered?* The gospel declares that God accepts us even before we love him. He never forces our love.

This love of God created the church as a community of persons who love God and one another. This free love, from God, for God, and among us is the foundation for the choir's song, and the *choir's practice*. The song is good. It is about grace.